Finding Jensen

A Path to Empathy Through Understanding

Jensen Dee Parker Chappell

For Amanda, Peyton, and Ada —

my family and my foundation, with whom this journey has been lovingly shared.

Praise for Finding Jensen

Readers across the country have shared how this story reshaped their understanding of empathy, identity, and what it means to truly see one another.

> *"Each chapter is a stepping stone toward greater self-awareness and emotional growth, offering a chance for reflection and personal development. Reading this book was like having a heart-to-heart with a wise friend. I'm already hoping for a part two—maybe on unconscious bias and how it shows up in workplaces and everyday life."*
> — Julia Moses

> *"Jensen shares openly with so much love for the audience. You can tell this book is written from a genuine desire to help you understand the experience of a trans person without judgment. What a gift."*
> — Mandy Hornbuckle

> *"Finding Jensen touched me deeply. It was like sitting down with a friend who finally put into words things I've always felt but didn't know how to say."*
> — Shandi

More than just a memoir, this book is a guide—a companion for anyone seeking to build connection through empathy, reflection, and courage.

Disclaimer

This book reflects the personal experiences, thoughts, and growth of the author. While every story is true to the author's perspective, memory is a human thing — subjective, layered, and personal. Some names, locations, and identifying details have been changed to respect the privacy of individuals involved.

This book is not a substitute for professional therapy, legal advice, or medical guidance. It's offered as an invitation to listen, reflect, and grow — not as a guide for diagnosis or decision-making.

Care Warning

Some of the stories in this book include references to gender dysphoria, grief, and moments of emotional struggle — including thoughts of self-harm. These experiences are shared with care and the hope that they will foster understanding, not cause harm.

If you find any part of this book emotionally overwhelming, please take breaks as needed. It's okay to pause. It's okay to skip a chapter. And it's more than okay to ask for support.

You are not alone. You are worthy of care — especially from yourself.

Table of Contents

Preface

This book is a journey — my journey — of coming into my own, understanding my identity as a transgender woman, and learning how to navigate a world that often struggles to understand people like me. But it's not just a memoir about being transgender. It's an invitation to grow empathy, to build bridges across difference, and to use language thoughtfully in a way that helps everyone feel more seen, heard, and respected.

When I first joined the DEI group at my workplace, it wasn't just to advocate for transgender inclusion, though that was part of it. I wanted to create a bridge between communities that often felt worlds apart. I wanted to show how understanding, when practiced with intention, can transform discomfort into compassion — and curiosity into allyship.

For me, understanding began as a survival skill. Long before I had the words to describe who I was, I learned to read people's reactions — the flicker of confusion in their eyes, the sudden shift to small talk when gender came too close to the surface. I picked up this skill early, in childhood, where small changes in tone or expression could speak louder than words. I became a kind of translator, working to explain my experience in ways that helped others connect with it. It was exhausting at times, but it was also powerful — turning awkward silences into moments of genuine connection.

That same skill — the willingness to understand and be understood — is at the heart of this book.

Through a mix of personal stories, lessons from my own missteps, and practical reflections, I hope to offer you tools to listen more deeply, speak more kindly, and build the kind of empathy that strengthens every relationship — not just with people like me, but with anyone whose experience is different from your own.

This isn't a book about perfection. It's not about getting everything right or never making mistakes. It's about learning, growing, and choosing to show up better each day. It's about how we recover when we slip up — and how even the smallest steps toward understanding can ripple farther than we realize.

Understanding is where it all begins.
It is the first step toward empathy.
And empathy is what makes true connection — and true allyship — possible.

I hope that by the end of this book, you'll see how powerful that first step can be. And how, by taking it, you just might change not only how you see others — but how you see yourself.

This book captures where I am now — in my story, my growth, and my understanding of what it means to connect across difference. But like all of us, I'm still learning.

You may have noticed the small sprout in a cup on the cover.

It's not just a decorative choice like you would see on an O'Reilly Book — it's a symbol I've carried with me through book signings and conversations, and one that holds quiet meaning throughout these pages.

To me, it represents the kind of growth that starts small — tender, uncertain, and in need of care. I once imagined it growing in a paper cup, but in my heart, it became an old coffee cup. A little worn. Maybe chipped. Not built for that purpose, but lovingly repurposed to hold something new.

I didn't set out to be an advocate or a leader. But people came to me with questions — sometimes halting, sometimes clumsy, but always genuine. They wanted to understand, even if they didn't know how to ask. In answering, I found a new purpose of my own.

This book is part of that. A little cup. A little sprout. If something here takes root in you, I hope you'll tend it gently and let it grow.

THE PERSONAL JOURNEY

This section is where I let you in.

It's where I take off the armor and share the messy, complicated, beautiful process of becoming myself. These chapters hold the weight of real moments—moments of fear, doubt, courage, and joy. They trace the arc of my gender journey, but also the ways it rippled into my relationships, my parenting, and my place in the world.

This part of the book isn't about being polished or resolved. It's about being honest.

Vulnerability lives here. And it's through that vulnerability that we begin to understand each other. Understanding, when met with care, becomes empathy. That's why I'm sharing this—not because every part of it is easy to tell, but because I believe empathy grows when we allow people to really see us.

At the end of each chapter, you'll find a small moment of reflection—a lesson or realization I took with me. These aren't wrapped in neat bows or grand conclusions. They're the kind of insights you carry quietly for a while before realizing how much they've shaped you.

Let these pieces of my story help you reflect on your own, and gain understanding of what it means to be myself—a transgender person who believes in the power of empathy.

The Color Green

The first time I dyed my hair, it was for a Halloween costume. I didn't expect to feel anything more than the thrill of a temporary change — the kind that washes out in a few weeks and leaves no trace.

But when I looked in the mirror and saw vibrant blue strands framing my face, I felt something I hadn't in a long time: confidence. Not the kind that comes from blending in or hitting all the marks that make life easier, but the kind that glows quietly beneath the surface, warming parts of me I hadn't yet named.

For a long time, I had lived in the margins of my own life, waiting for permission to take up space and be seen.

That moment made me realize: growth doesn't need permission. It just needs the courage to push through.
That's what coming into my own felt like — finding those cracks and allowing myself to grow through them, even when it felt easier to stay hidden.

The blue didn't last long. Not long after, my partner Amanda and I found our current hair colorist, someone who could translate the shades in my mind into reality.

One of my longest color trends was a blend of toucan-like hues, bright and tropical, inspired by a Super Mario shirt I owned. The shirt itself was green and showed a bowl of "super power-up cereal," filled with mushrooms, stars, and flowers. Seeing those bright, playful tones reflected back at me felt like stepping out of grayscale and into full technicolor.

Green has always been my favorite color. Maybe that's why the blue never stuck for long. Green is the color of growth, of life pushing through cracks in the concrete, of things that thrive against the odds. That's part of why it resonates with me so much.

Green is also Luigi from Super Mario, my favorite character — always a little overshadowed but steady, loyal, and capable of surprising heroics when given the chance. It's a color that feels like becoming, never fully settled but constantly moving forward.

Each dye session became a ritual, a way to shed the dull layers of pretending and embrace the parts of me that felt authentic.

The colors were a rebellion against invisibility — a way to say, *"I'm here,"* without needing to find the words.

The more I saw myself in the mirror, the more I wanted to explore.

Clothes became less about fitting in and more about feeling right.
I tried different styles, finding pieces that made me feel seen instead of hidden.

It was a slow unfolding, but each choice felt a little more honest than the last.

The real turning point came on an anniversary trip to Little Rock, Arkansas.

Amanda and I were celebrating another year together — years marked by love, growth, and the kind of honesty that takes time to build.

I found myself sitting in a small salon, nervous but determined, watching as a nail technician carefully painted each nail. The polish was color-changing — from a bright fluorescent yellow when warm to a dark, almost forest green when cold.

It felt like a small rebellion, a quiet transformation.

Amanda smiled at me across the room, her eyes warm and steady. And in that moment, I knew I could keep exploring — because I wasn't doing it alone.

Looking at my reflection that night — nails shifting colors, hair bright with the hues of a Super Mario power-up — I saw a glimpse of the person I was becoming.
Someone more me than I had ever been before.

Self-realization comes in many forms, often in ways we least expect.

For me, it started with a bottle of hair dye and the courage to see what might happen if I stopped hiding.

It's a reminder that we shouldn't stifle the ways people seek to understand themselves, even when those ways seem small or unimportant at first.

Every step toward becoming is a step worth celebrating.

When we make space for people to grow, to experiment, to discover who they are, we're practicing empathy at its most powerful.

The Nightgown

The first time I realized my gender, I didn't have the words to describe
it.
I was too young to understand why that moment mattered — or why
it would linger in my mind for years afterward, resurfacing every time
I looked in the mirror and didn't quite recognize the person staring
back.

All I knew was that something about it felt right, even though every
other sign pointed to it being wrong.

It started as an act of spite.

My uncles were visiting that day, tossing insults back and forth like
playing cards, their voices rough and careless.
They didn't see anything wrong with the words they used — words
that cut through the room with edges sharpened by repetition.

My mom heard them too.
Her jaw tightened, her eyes narrowing with the kind of anger that
doesn't raise its voice.

She didn't snap or lecture.
Instead, she went quiet, her eyes glinting with the sort of defiance only
a mother can muster.

She took my twin brother and me by the hand and led us into her
bedroom.
Before I understood what was happening, she was pulling out nightgowns — soft, pastel things that smelled faintly of fabric softener and

her favorite perfume.
She slid one over my head, adjusted the hem, and slipped boots onto my feet.

I remember how the fabric felt, light and unfamiliar, brushing against my legs.
She leaned in close, lipstick poised, and whispered, *"Hold still."*

When she was done, she stepped back, her eyes bright with something that looked almost like pride.
"Now," she said, her voice sweet and venomous all at once, *"go show your uncles."*

I don't remember what my brother felt at that moment, but I remember what I felt:
A strange mix of terror and longing.

My dad was in the living room, eyes fixed on the wall as if by staring hard enough, he could pretend the whole thing wasn't happening.
My uncles fell silent the moment they saw us, their mouths twisting with disgust, their faces red with the kind of anger that boils over and burns everything in its path.

I should have felt ashamed.
I should have ripped the nightgown off and hidden until it was safe to come out.

But I didn't.

Beneath the fear and the flush of my cheeks, there was something else — something that settled in my chest and whispered *yes.*

I knew it wasn't socially acceptable.
I knew boys weren't supposed to wear nightgowns or lipstick or anything that made them look too soft, too bright.

But for a few moments, none of that mattered.

For the first time, I didn't feel like I was pretending to be someone I wasn't.

I didn't have the language for it yet — the words would come later, a slow unraveling of syllables that made sense of the quiet ache that had been with me for so long.

But in that moment, I felt something fundamental.
And it's something I would understand more clearly as I grew:
That the person I saw in the mirror wasn't a mistake.
That maybe, if I followed that feeling — if I dared to let it grow instead of burying it — I could find a way to become who I was meant to be.

That day lit a spark.

And even though it would take years to fan that spark into a flame, it was the first time I realized that there might be another way to live — one where I didn't have to pretend.

My mom's act of defiance that day wasn't just about lipstick and nightgowns.
It was her way of teaching my uncles a lesson about the weight of their words — how the slurs and crude remarks they threw around so casually could cut into their own family without them even realizing it.

I won't ever know if she got the outcome she wanted.
My uncles weren't ready to learn that lesson that day, and they passed away before I ever came out.

Nevertheless, that moment stayed with me, unfolding slowly into a deeper understanding of myself.

Sometimes, the lessons that don't land where we intend find a way to grow in someone else.

If nothing else, it taught me that defiance can be an act of love — and that the courage to push back, even quietly, can change a life.

The First to Know

My mom was the first person to know.
Long before I could articulate what I was feeling, before I had the words to tell anyone else, I told her.
It wasn't planned, just a moment that unfolded unexpectedly, one I hadn't seen coming even in my most honest dreams.

Those dreams had been a constant for as long as I could remember.
In them, I was always a girl.
Sometimes the details blurred and shifted — settings I didn't recognize, faces that felt familiar but weren't — but that part never changed.
I'd wake up in the gray light of morning with the ghost of those dreams clinging to me, a quiet ache that lingered long after I opened my eyes.
I never told anyone about them. Not at first.

Then came the day my mom found one of her bras in my room.
I can still see the way she held it, fingers pinched at the straps, eyebrows pulled together in confusion.

"What is this doing in here?" she asked, her voice carefully neutral, as if already bracing herself for whatever explanation I might give.

I knew what she was thinking — that it was the sort of thing boys did when they were curious, that it was just a phase or a joke or something she could laugh off later.
But that wasn't it at all.

I opened my mouth, heart pounding so loudly I could barely hear my own words.
And then, before I could think better of it, I told her the truth.

About the dreams.

About the way I felt when I looked in the mirror and couldn't recognize myself.

About how it wasn't a joke or a phase or some half-formed curiosity.

It was something I couldn't explain, but couldn't ignore either — an ache that had settled deep and refused to go away.

She didn't say anything.

No sigh, no angry words, not even the soft, awkward laughter of someone trying to smooth things over.

Just silence, heavy and cold, settling into the room like winter.

In that silence, something inside me shrank back, folding itself small and tight, hidden deep where no one could find it.

Where I could pretend it didn't exist at all.

That silence sealed it.

That was the moment I knew I couldn't let it back out.

Whatever I was feeling, whatever name it had, couldn't be okay if it left my mom speechless.

So I locked it away, quiet and deep, and threw every wall I could find around it.

For years, I kept it hidden, even from myself.

I buried it under schoolwork, distractions, the slow work of growing up.

I learned to play the part, to live the life I thought I was supposed to want.

And I did. I fell in love. I got married.

It wasn't until then, well after the wedding and deep into the life my partner Amanda and I were building together, that those walls began to crack.

We were having late-night conversations about sexuality, hours of words spoken in the dark, the kind that can only exist between two people who have promised each other forever.

In that space, the feelings I had buried for so long began to surface — hesitant and uncertain, but there.

By then, it was too late to share those truths with my mom.
She passed away around the same time my uncles did, before I ever found the words to tell her who I was becoming.

In her last weeks, after the stroke had left her mostly paralyzed and cancer had taken its toll, I found myself helping her shower.

She was a modest woman, even then, trying to hide herself behind trembling hands and lowered eyes.
I could see the insecurity in the way she turned away, ashamed to be seen by one of her "sons" in her full, naked femininity.

I tried to soothe her, to break the tension with a gentle, *"Moma, stop hiding yourself. It's not like I haven't seen a naked body before."*
But the truth was, in that moment, I connected with her more deeply than I ever had — except for maybe the day I first confessed my secret to her.

I was there in her last days, carrying the weight of everything I hadn't said, standing on the verge of exploring my femininity as an adult.
That's when I realized that maybe her silence hadn't been the end of the story.
Maybe, this time, I wouldn't have to lock the door behind me.

Looking back, I see that the silence that day wasn't just about the words my mom didn't say. It was about the truth she wasn't ready to understand.

Maybe that's the hardest part of being honest with others: knowing that sometimes they won't have the space to hold what you're telling them.

In a small town in West Texas, the idea of being transgender wasn't something she could have wrapped her mind around — especially not from the little boy she had raised.

I never got the chance to tell her with the confidence and understanding I have now.
That loss taught me a hard lesson: we don't always get a second chance to share our truth or help others understand.

Silence leaves its own scars.
But finding the courage to speak, even when it feels too late, is still a risk worth taking. Because sometimes, the act of saying the words out loud is how we begin to heal.

Missteps

It's hard to find the right time to tell the truth.
I used to think there would be a perfect moment — one where the words would come easy, and no one would flinch or frown or look away.
I waited years for that moment, rehearsing the words until they were smooth as river stones.

But when the truth finally came out, it was at the worst possible time.

Amanda was pregnant when I first started transitioning — slowly and quietly, testing the waters when no one was looking.
I knew it was poorly timed.
I knew we should have been focusing on her and the baby, preparing for the late nights and lullabies and all the chaos that was coming.
But the feeling I'd been holding back for years refused to stay buried.

The first time I pulled on a pair of leggings, the fabric was soft and snug against my legs.
I felt a jolt of recognition so sharp it was like finding a missing piece of myself.
It was a small thing, almost nothing at all, but it was enough to pry open a door I'd been holding shut for so long my hands were shaking.

But it was the shoes that really did it.

The way they clicked on the tile.
The way they made me stand a little taller and feel a little lighter.
There was something powerful about that sound — a quiet rebellion with every step.
The heels felt amazing, shifting my posture and changing the way my

figure felt.

For a few moments, I could pretend that the person in the mirror was real — that I was real.

Amanda, though, felt like I was upstaging her.

Like I had made it all about me when we should have been focusing on her and the life growing inside her.

And I understood.

I really did.

But understanding didn't stop the ache of wanting to be seen, to be known for who I was — even if I couldn't say it yet.

So I started hiding things.

I packed leggings and shoes into a bag and tucked it under the spare tire in the trunk of my car, where no one would think to look.

In the mornings, I'd change before walking into work, feeling the click of heels on tile and the whisper of fabric swaying around my legs.

For those few hours, I could breathe.

But hiding wasn't enough.

I started leaving little things out — quiet tests to see how Amanda might react.

I'd wear my makeup just a bit too long, let the eyeliner smudge at the corners until it was almost obvious.

I'd keep the leggings on a little longer after getting home, wondering if she'd notice or say anything.

And then, finally, the shoes.

That was the last straw.

I had promised I'd gotten rid of them.

Technically, I had.

That pair was gone.

But I couldn't resist buying another, nearly identical pair of women's boots.

The look on her face when she found out was worse than any argument.
Disbelief. Hurt.
The kind of silence that can shatter glass.

It was a breach of trust, and I knew it the moment I saw her expression.

That moment felt like the ground opening up beneath me.
I tried to explain, but the words tangled and tripped over each other — too many apologies and not enough honesty.

All I could think about was how the heels had felt.
How right they had been.
How sure.

But that didn't matter in the silence that followed.

Looking back, I can see the missteps for what they were — stumbles, not failures.
At the time, it felt like all I was doing was falling.
But therapy taught me the power of perspective — that sometimes it takes an outside voice to help us ask the right questions and find the courage to admit when we're wrong.

I learned that it's not enough to just say sorry; you have to follow it with action.
It's about asking, *"How can I help?"* or *"How can I make things better?"*
Or, hardest of all, knowing what you need to do and saying, *"I understand."*

Honesty isn't just about sharing who you are — it's about rebuilding trust when it's been broken.

It's about showing up, again and again, with the willingness to be better.

Even missteps, I've found, can teach us how to walk a little more honestly, a little more bravely, toward who we're meant to be.

Our Story, Not My Story

We both thought it might be the end.
There were nights when the silence between us felt so thick I could hardly breathe.
Words sat half-formed and caught in my throat because I wasn't sure what would come out if I opened my mouth.
Neither of us could look too far ahead without flinching.

There was no easy way to untangle all the what-ifs.
What if I did transition?
What if she couldn't see me the same way?
What if the person I was becoming wasn't someone she wanted to stay married to?

I was terrified of losing her.
The thought of Amanda leaving was a weight in my chest that never really went away.
I loved her so much that imagining a life without her felt like trying to breathe underwater.
It was cold and suffocating and impossible.

But at the same time, the idea of pretending to be someone I wasn't — of locking those feelings back up, throwing away the key, and going back to the way things used to be — felt just as unbearable.

My trans friends didn't understand it.
They'd ask, voices sharp with confusion, *"What is up with you? Why are you staying with her? She should let you live your authentic self!"*

And it was true.

Of course it was true.
I knew, deep down, that they were right — that living half a life wasn't really living at all.

But it was so much more complicated than that.

Because it wasn't just about authenticity.
It was about Amanda.
It was about the way her eyes crinkled at the corners when she laughed, the way she could read my moods without me saying a word, the way her hand felt in mine even on the worst days.

It was about the life we had built together — brick by brick, promise by promise.

My identity wasn't something I could lock away anymore.
But neither was my love for her.

The truth was, there was plenty of hurt to go around.

Amanda wasn't just hurt by the idea of me transitioning.
She was hurt by the secrets, by the things I'd hidden, by the way I couldn't bring myself to tell her.
And I was hurt by the silence that followed each time I tried and failed to say the words out loud.

It felt like tearing pieces off each other — slow and jagged — neither of us sure if there would be anything left when we were done.

In those quiet moments, alone in the dark with nothing but my thoughts, I couldn't help but wonder what was wrong with me.

Why couldn't I just go back to the way it was before — before the makeup and the leggings and the shoes?
Why did I have to push so hard, dig so deep, even when I could see

the hurt it was causing?

If I really loved Amanda, shouldn't I have been able to stop — to turn back before everything fell apart?

That was when Amanda started therapy.

She didn't go to figure me out.
She went to figure herself out — to understand her own identity and what it would mean if I transitioned.

It reminded me of that subreddit, *Am I the Asshole?*
Not because she was looking for a verdict — but because she was trying to find the truth beneath the guilt and confusion.
She was trying to understand if her feelings were fair, or if she was being unfair to me — or to herself.

That's the thing about being married while transitioning.
The story isn't just yours anymore.
It stops being *I* and starts being *us* — our past, our present, our future, all tangled together in a way that makes it impossible to pull one thread without unraveling the rest.

Every conversation felt like walking a tightrope — trying to balance my need to be true to myself with her need to understand who she was married to.

In therapy, Amanda started asking herself questions she'd never considered before.

What did it make her if I transitioned?
Did it change the way she saw herself — the way the world saw her?
Did it change what it meant to love me?

The questions came slow and careful, like stepping through a minefield.

But she kept asking.

And in those late-night conversations — when it was dark and quiet and there was nowhere to hide — we started to find new words.

Words that made room for both of us.
Words that didn't pit my truth against hers or force us to pick sides.

It was messy and raw and terrifying.
But it was ours.

Looking back, I think that was the real turning point. It wasn't the clothes or the makeup or the shoes. It was the realization that this wasn't just my story.
It was ours.

Empathy isn't just about understanding someone else's truth.
Sometimes, it is about making room for two truths to exist side by side — without canceling each other out.

It is about finding new words when the old ones don't fit — and being willing to rewrite the story together, even when it hurts.

If I've learned anything, it's that love isn't about erasing yourself to make someone else comfortable.

It's about building a life where both of you can grow — even if it means tearing down old walls to start over together.

Making a Name for Myself

Finding the right name felt like searching for a bridge between my past and my true self.
It was a way to honor where I came from while stepping fully into who I was becoming.

Keeping my initials was important.
It was a way of maintaining a thread of continuity — a subtle reminder that while my name was changing, the core of who I was remained.

I sifted through over fifty names, balancing each one on a scale of gender neutrality or a slight feminine tilt.
Nothing felt quite right until I stumbled upon Jensen — inspired by a red-headed female character from a book series Amanda and I were reading at the time.
Fittingly, I was sporting red hair then too.

Scandinavian in descent, its meaning — "descendant of John" — felt almost fated, a way to acknowledge the name my parents gave me without denying the truth of who I am.
Its connection to a character from a book Amanda and I were reading only made it feel more fitting, like a signpost I'd been waiting to see.

In that moment, I knew.
Jensen was the name I had been searching for.

I've never seen my given name as a dead name.
To me, it was a gift from my parents — a reflection of their hopes and love at the time of my birth.
Even though it no longer identified me, it was a part of my story — a

chapter that led me to Jensen.

There's a lot of power in names — in choosing one's own identity — but there's also power in honoring the journey that brought you there. Recognizing my given name as a gift helped me feel less like I was discarding my past and more like I was building on it.

It's worth pausing to explain what a dead name is.

For many trans people, a dead name is the name given at birth that no longer represents them.
Being called by that name can be deeply painful — a reminder of a life they've left behind and a version of themselves that didn't feel authentic.
That's why it's considered impolite — even harmful — to ask someone what their dead name was.
It's a question that can drag someone back into a past they've worked hard to move beyond.

For me, my given name isn't a dead name.
It's a part of my past that I acknowledge without resentment.
But that's not true for everyone, and it's important to understand why some trans people need that part of their history to stay in the past.

Early on, I even found myself reverting back to my given name, John, in moments of frustration or when I would mess up.
It was an old habit of referring to myself in the third person.
It's something I hardly ever do anymore, but at the time, it felt like a safety net — a way to ease the discomfort of redefining myself.
Today, it feels almost weird to hear my given name spoken about me or to me.

Navigating my name change with my family back in my hometown was, and still is, hard.

At work, the process was so quick and everyone seemed ready to embrace it.

I submitted the request to change my name at work over Christmas break, assuming it would be processed in the new year.
I wanted to start fresh with the new calendar, give people time to adjust, and give myself time to prepare.

What I didn't expect was for it to go through the very next day.

Seeing my email change overnight, signatures updated, and people addressing me as Jensen before I'd even had my morning coffee was surreal.
I was one of the first at my workplace to navigate the preferred name system without a legal change, which led to a flurry of complications. Emails bounced, permissions broke, and I spent the next few weeks untangling technical knots while trying to navigate the emotional weight of suddenly being Jensen everywhere.

For every colleague who welcomed the name change with open arms, pronouns were a different story.

I was using They/Them pronouns at this time in my transition — uncertain if I wanted to present femininely or embrace womanhood yet.
I felt nearly like I was squatting in a space I hadn't earned — or as if I were telling people a lie because I had been considered male all my life.

I was also playing with gender a lot — something I still do on occasion.

Jensen went over surprisingly well.
Only every now and again did someone revert to my previous name, mostly those who had known me the longest.

But They/Them pronouns were a struggle for many.
It wasn't out of malice; it was more about old habits and the challenge of adjusting to something unfamiliar.
Still, most people were very intentional about it — and that made all the difference.

I used my 1-on-1s as teaching moments for my manager, who was fully supportive but had never dealt with a situation like mine before — someone coming out and redefining themselves while continuing to work at the same place.

Those conversations were a chance to educate and to share what was helpful and what wasn't.

It was exhausting, but every time I heard someone address me as Jensen, it was a small victory — a reminder that I was here, fully present as my true self.

I went a couple of years without officially changing my name.
The act of doing it was daunting.
I tried a couple of times to handle it myself but always found the process overwhelming.

In the end, I hired a lawyer to help me put the steps together.
Due to my means, I had the privilege of proceeding that way.
The lawyer gave me a game plan and solid steps on how to gather the documents and get it all done.

The official act of changing my name and gender marker on my court order, driver's license, and social security felt less like a final step and more like the beginning of everything else.

Holding those documents in my hands was a validation — not just from the world, but from myself.

In that moment, Jensen wasn't just a name.
It was a declaration of my right to exist authentically.

The name you are given is something you grow into — something you mold yourself around until it fits.

But a name you choose for yourself is different.

It's yours to define — to shape into something that reflects who you really are.

It's like the perfect set of heels.
It raises you up, makes you look good, and fits just right.

In choosing my name, I was able to claim my identity with confidence and refused to be hidden or defined by anyone else's expectations.

If I've learned anything, it's that choosing your name is one of the first and bravest steps toward choosing yourself.

One Street Over

When Amanda and I bought our house, we weren't just moving into a home — we were stepping into a neighborhood that, at the time, was barely on the edge of the metroplex.
Back then, houses were selling before the sun even set.

We got ours thanks to a bit of luck, a dedicated realtor, and a heartfelt note to the sellers about our dreams for raising a family.

It felt like a fresh start.

On the first day in the new house, we managed to hit our neighbor's car parked in the street.
Not exactly the grand entrance we hoped for.

But in a strange twist, that moment of awkwardness turned into a bonding experience.
We laughed about it — eventually — and found ourselves welcomed in.
Barbecues, neighborhood chats, invites to gatherings.

For a little while, we were part of the "in" crowd.

Then the pandemic hit.
Everything slowed down.

People withdrew, physically and emotionally.
By the time folks started stepping out again, something had shifted.

I had come out.
And the invitations stopped.

We weren't outright shunned.
No one said anything cruel to our faces.

But the silence was loud.
Some of our neighbors had always leaned more conservative, but now the political differences stood out in sharper contrast.

Conversations stopped happening.
Doors stayed closed.
We felt it — the quiet distancing.

Then came the fight over solar panels.

Texas has a law that protects homeowners' rights to install solar, but our HOA had crafted just enough rules to let neighbors block it if they didn't like how it looked.
One of our neighbors didn't want to see them from his side of the street and made that known in no uncertain terms.

He was the kind of neighbor who always had an unsolicited lesson ready.
Every conversation was as if I were incapable of understanding on my own, and nothing I said could change that.

To add insult to injury, not only did he treat me like I lacked any sense, but he could never even remember my given name — or my chosen name.
Instead, he called me "Jeff."

Where that came from, who knows.
It was his way of reducing me to a stereotype he clung to.

It got heated — more than it should have — and we exchanged some words I wish had gone unsaid.
Another neighbor witnessed the whole thing, standing in her driveway

across the street.

I felt awful.
Not just about the fight, but about how everything felt so tense and brittle.

I walked over to apologize, to explain that it wasn't about disrespect — just frustration, built-up and misdirected.
We had a brief moment of calm, a few words exchanged.

Afterward, I headed back toward my house, just about to walk through the garage door, when I heard a voice behind me — concerned, but powerful.

> "I love all my neighbors, but don't you know you're going to hell for what you're doing to your body?"

There was no pause, no softening.
Just a sermon.

"One day," she continued, "you're going to have to get right with the Almighty."

I didn't lash out.
I took a breath.

And I told her what I believed — that science and lived experience shape my understanding of gender and identity.
That sex, gender, and expression exist on a spectrum.

That I don't believe in a being watching every move, passing judgment from above.
I believe in energy, in luck, in the mystery of it all.

She shook her head the entire time.

31

Not a subtle shake — a sharp, insistent one, as if every word I said was a personal affront.

I ended our conversation with this:

"I believe people are free to follow whatever faith gives them peace. But your belief doesn't get to define me — any more than mine should define you.
If you ever want to talk about what it means to be transgender, really talk, I'm here."

She didn't say anything back.

For a while, we avoided each other.
And I won't lie — it hurt.

I tried not to let it, but it did.
You want to believe that being open, being kind, being yourself is enough.

But sometimes, it still costs you something.

And then, after a couple of years, she started waving again.
Saying hello.
Making small talk as if nothing had ever happened.

Did she accept me?
I don't think so.

But maybe — just maybe — seeing me live my life, raise my kids, smile at my wife, and show up day after day helped her unlearn whatever fear or judgment she carried.
Maybe it cracked open something she didn't even know was shut.

That's not the whole story, though.

Because while some neighbors pulled away, others stepped in.
As our daughter started school, our community expanded.

We met other parents — moms especially — who didn't blink when they met our family.
They welcomed us into birthday parties, park meetups, and school functions.

They treated us like, well... people.

And when the PTA reached out and asked if I'd consider joining, specifically to help with diversity and inclusion efforts, I felt something shift again.

I realized I had been bracing myself for rejection — expecting cold shoulders and quiet exits.
But instead, I found new hands reaching out, inviting me in.

Some people in our neighborhood may always see the world a certain way.
But this neighborhood is bigger than them.

And what I've learned is that acceptance doesn't always come from where you expect it.
Sometimes it lives one street over — not in miles, but in mindset.

That's how it felt with her.
We were just across the street from each other, close enough to wave from our driveways.

But emotionally, it felt like we lived in different worlds, as if I had moved just one street over from where I used to belong.

But across that invisible divide, something surprising happened.

And that's the version of community I want to believe in — not the one defined by sameness, but the one we build by choosing to care anyway.

Because even if we don't all live on the same street, we still share the same neighborhood.

A Child's Perception

Peyton was the one who really made the decision.
We gave her the choice of how she wanted to represent us to her classmates.

I was still in the middle of searching for gender stability — exploring the idea of being non-binary or gender fluid.
Amanda was always Mommy.
There was never any question about that.
She was adamant about having that name because she birthed our kids.

The idea of me stepping into that space made her apprehensive — maybe because it felt like a line that was hers alone — and honestly, I didn't want it either.

At the time, saying I was a woman didn't feel entirely accurate.
It still doesn't sometimes.
Gender is a spectrum, but we talk about it in absolutes so often that it feels like there's no room for anything in between.

I wasn't ready to step into the label of "Mom" when I was still figuring out what fit.

So we explored other names that didn't lean one way or the other.
Agender options like Zaza or Parpar.
I think we took the word "parent" and disassembled it in every way possible, trying to find something that felt right.

Peyton listened, head tilted with that wide-eyed focus that kids get

when they're trying to solve a puzzle.
When we mentioned breaking down "parent" into parts, she perked up at one name in particular.

"Riri," she said, testing the sound of it like a secret.

Up until that moment, I was Daddy.
Even though I looked like a woman most of the time, Peyton never stumbled over it.
She would grab my hand in public, look right at me, and call me Daddy without a second thought.

But when she said *"Riri,"* something clicked for both of us.
It was soft and warm, a name without sharp edges.

From that moment on, I was Riri — and we never looked back.

Not long after, in that same year, in kindergarten, Peyton explained to her classmates without a hint of hesitation.
She told them she had two moms — that one of them had a low voice like a boy and some boyish features.

Kids are funny that way — so direct and practical about things adults stumble over.
She said it plainly, with the kind of confidence that only a child can have — as if it were the simplest thing in the world.

Ada has never known anything different.
To her, I've always been Riri.

From the time she could form sentences, she corrected people who called me Dad or used the wrong pronouns.
It was never confrontational — just a gentle correction with that straightforward confidence kids have.

"Don't you mean my mom, Riri?" she would ask, head tilted slightly, as if the mistake was simple to fix.
There was never any doubt in her voice.

My children are both my little advocates — fierce and unflinching in their love.

I've always tried to teach them that families come in all shapes and sizes — two moms, two dads, one mom, one dad, a grandparent, even just a chosen guardian.
These are all shapes of families — and not a single one of them is wrong.

Kids have a way of accepting things as they are without getting stuck on labels — at least until the world teaches them to question what doesn't fit neatly into a box.

Peyton and Ada didn't need explanations or definitions.
They just knew who I was and spoke it into being with a kind of simple, fearless love that only children seem to have.

It makes me wonder how different things might be if we taught kids to question social norms instead of accepting them blindly — if we taught them to ask why people believe what they do instead of just teaching them to believe it too.

Hearing *"Riri"* for the first time felt like being seen without having to explain — like a gift I didn't know I needed.

It was a reminder that identity isn't just about choosing who you are — it's also about trusting the people who see you clearly.

Sometimes, the greatest gift we can receive is to be named by those who love us — without hesitation or conditions.

Those same loving children also learn everything from watching us and from interacting with their peers.

If we teach them hate, they will learn hate.
But if instead we teach them acceptance — and to ask thoughtful questions — we will be providing them the tools for a bright future.

The Weight of a Voice

"There's a difference between hearing someone's voice and actually hearing who they are."

For many trans people, voice training is about far more than learning a new skill.
It's survival.
It's safety.
It's the difference between being seen or being questioned, between blending in or standing out in ways that can feel dangerous.

Few things expose the fragile edges of gender dysphoria more than the sound of your own voice echoing back at you — especially when it doesn't match who you know yourself to be.

For some, it becomes the sharpest weapon dysphoria wields — a constant reminder that no matter how you look, how you dress, or how you carry yourself, there's still this one thing you can't hide.

Your voice can betray you before you even step into the room.

That's what makes voice dysphoria so cruel.
It isn't something you can always control.
It follows you everywhere — in phone calls, video meetings, customer service interactions, and casual conversations.
It's inescapable.

And every time someone hears you and makes the wrong assumption, it chips away at you.
It can turn the most mundane parts of life into exhausting, anxious

moments.

The worst part is that it isn't just about how you hear yourself.
It's about how the world reacts to you.

Dysphoria becomes the voice inside you whispering, *"They'll never see you the way you see yourself."*
And when strangers misgender you based on your voice, that whisper grows louder.

That hasn't entirely been my experience.

I do feel some discomfort with my voice.
There are moments when that flicker of dysphoria creeps in.
But it's not the loud, constant presence that it is for so many others.

For me, the real weight of it shows up when other people interpret my voice in a way that doesn't match who I am.
It's how deeply my voice is coded as male — how easily it triggers misgendering, even when everything else about me reads as feminine.

That's when dysphoria feels like an adversary — when someone else's assumption turns something as simple as speaking into a reminder that I still live in a world that doesn't always see me clearly.

I'm privileged in many ways.
I've lived in environments where my safety hasn't depended on my voice "passing."
That's not a small thing.
Many people don't have that safety.

Still, even in a safe environment, there are moments when the stakes feel heavier than they should.
A phone call.
A drive-thru window.

An introduction over Zoom.

And just like that, the sound of your voice is enough for someone to assign you an identity you didn't choose.

The irony is, I've always loved voices.
I've been doing impressions and silly accents since I was a kid.
Bedtime stories in my house were never read in my normal voice.

SpongeBob Goes to the Doctor just isn't the same unless I'm doing my very best SpongeBob, Patrick, and Mr. Krabs.

So I thought I'd have a head start when I began voice training.

I didn't.

Doing a convincing woman's voice isn't about mimicry.
It's not just pitch.
It's cadence, resonance, pacing, and variation.
It's how emotion rides the rhythm of your speech.

And even when you learn those things, you can still be misgendered — because of how people have been conditioned to hear gender.

I worked with Seattle Voice Lab, and they gave me tools.

Not a mask.
Not something to hide behind.
Just skills I can choose to use when I want to move through the world with less friction.

Along the way, I learned something I didn't expect.
I didn't want to mimic someone else's voice or pretend to be something I'm not.

I even tried once or twice, leaning into a voice I thought sounded

feminine — only to have Amanda tell me it didn't sound like me.
She was right.
It felt hollow — like I was covering something up instead of revealing who I really was.

So I leaned into what they taught me.

I learned how to soften my cadence, how to shift my speech patterns, how to let go of tension and speak in a way that felt more like me. Not to perform, but to be understood.

I don't need to perform femininity all the time.
But I use what I've learned when it helps me avoid being misunderstood or misgendered.

Sometimes I just want to order a coffee without explaining who I am.

That's the lesson I want people to hear — not just about voice training, but about empathy.

The struggle isn't really about a voice at all.
It's about being caught in the tension between how you know yourself and how the world insists on seeing you.

Dysphoria doesn't just live in the mirror or in the sound of your own voice.
It lives in every assumption, every question, every moment someone gets you wrong.

Empathy doesn't require you to know what that feels like firsthand.

It's about recognizing that for some people, the simple act of speaking out loud takes courage.
It's about seeing how exhausting it is to wonder if the world will actually listen to you — or if it will only hear what it expects to hear.

And it's about understanding that when someone is fighting to find their voice, they aren't just hoping to be heard.
They're hoping to finally be known.

EMPATHY IN ACTION

I hope the stories in the first part, *The Personal Journey*, of this book helped you understand a little more about the truth I live — and the weight and wonder that comes with it. I believe deeply in the power of storytelling to ground people in understanding. When we truly see one another, empathy has room to grow — and that empathy can be the first step in learning about communities like mine that are so often misunderstood.

That part opened a window into the messy, beautiful, often complicated work of being seen — of finding the language to name your truth, and the courage to share it.
It wasn't always easy, but I hope it felt real.

While those stories are personal, they are also an invitation: to understand what it feels like to carry a life that doesn't always fit the mold, and to begin building the kind of empathy that understanding makes possible.

This next part is where the lens shifts — where we start to explore what we *do* with that understanding. It blends reflection with practical insight. Think of it as a guide, not a rulebook — something you can return to when you're unsure how to respond, how to repair, or how to show up.

These aren't lessons from a perfect teacher — just experiences from someone who's had to learn, stumble, and grow.

Each chapter ends with a reflection to help you pause, process, and apply. Let them meet you where you are. Let them stretch you a little farther than you thought you could go.

Because empathy, when we choose to live it, doesn't just change how we see the world.
It changes how we move in it.

Empathy is a Skill, Not a Trait

Empathy isn't something you're born with. It's something you build, one conversation, one mistake, one uncomfortable realization at a time.

What Is Empathy?

At its core, empathy is the ability to understand and share the feelings of another person.

That's the textbook definition. But in real life, empathy isn't something sterile or academic. It's something you feel, and more importantly, something you practice.

Empathy is what happens in the pause.
The moment right before you respond, when you quiet your own perspective just long enough to let someone else's in.

It's not about knowing all the facts or having lived the same experience. It's about being willing to feel with someone, even when you don't fully understand the path that brought them there.

I see this all the time with my kids. It can be so easy to dismiss the way they feel — getting upset over not getting the candy they want or having to go to bed. From the outside, it seems so small.

But small doesn't mean unimportant.

My daughter has a stuffed bunny she's deeply attached to. It's not particularly fancy. It was given to her by an ex-girlfriend of her uncle, someone who isn't even in our lives anymore. But to her, that bunny means the whole world.

She takes it everywhere, then forgets where she left it. And when bedtime comes and she realizes it's missing, it feels like the end of the world.

The easy reaction would be to sigh and think, "It's just one bunny. You have six other ones."

But I have to stop.
I have to pause.
And in that moment, I remind myself: if something I truly loved — like her — went missing, how would I feel? Probably just as distraught. Just as heartbroken. So overwhelmed that logic would vanish, and all that would remain would be feeling.

Empathy doesn't mean minimizing someone's pain because it looks different than ours.
It means recognizing that their feelings are real, even if we wouldn't feel the same way in their place.

It means remembering that what matters isn't how big or small the problem seems to us. It's how big or small it feels to them.

Empathy doesn't require agreement.
It doesn't require fixing things.
It doesn't even require having the right words.

It only asks that you be present, curious, and open.

Because when we choose to feel with someone instead of looking away, we give them something deeply human: the feeling of being seen.

That's empathy.

Empathy Isn't Just "Being Nice"

Empathy is often confused with kindness or politeness. But it's not the same thing.

Here's the difference:

- **Kindness** is about what you do.

- **Sympathy** is about how you feel for someone.

- **Empathy** is about how well you can feel with someone.

You can be kind without being empathetic. You can even feel sorry for someone without ever stepping into their shoes.

Empathy goes deeper. It asks you to pause, listen, and imagine what it's like to be someone else, in that exact moment.
It's less about saying, *"That sounds hard,"* and more about asking, *"What is it like to be in your shoes right now?"*

That question has grounded me so many times in my life. One moment that stands out was with a coworker who often communicated in a way that felt cold and mechanical — very brief, very factual, almost like they were trying to strip away any emotion. At first glance, it would come off as curt or even condescending.

We were dealing with a bug that had cropped up in a feature they were building, and as we exchanged findings, they pointed out something in our code and added, *"Oh right, and you aren't tagging your releases."* I could feel my jaw clench. My first instinct was to fire back — be just as blunt, maybe even call them out publicly. I was frustrated. It felt like an unnecessary dig.

But I stopped.

I asked myself that question: *What is it like to be in their shoes right now?*

And I realized, this person is brilliant, yes. But they've never had any formal communication training. Their brevity isn't meant to be rude. It's just how they're wired. Somewhere along the way, that style had become "just how they are," even if it occasionally left friction behind.

So instead of retaliating, I leaned into empathy. I messaged them privately and said, *"Hey, I really want to help you with your communication style."* I used non-violent language to express how their message made me feel and offered a few suggestions for softening it — small tweaks that could build trust instead of eroding it.

At first, they didn't get it. They didn't even realize their communication was a problem.

But because I chose empathy over ego, I was able to offer insight they'd never received — and we left the conversation with more mutual respect than when it started.

Empathy isn't about being nice.
It's about choosing connection when disconnection would be easier.
It's about understanding that someone's behavior often makes more sense when you're willing to look beneath the surface.

How Empathy Grows

If empathy is a skill, how do we actually build it?

It doesn't start with knowing the right thing to say or mastering perfect timing. It starts with intention. With the willingness to pause, notice, and respond in ways that stretch us outside of our own perspective.

There are three key practices that grow empathy over time.

Curiosity

Empathy begins with curiosity — the gentle, open-ended desire to understand someone else's experience. Not to fix them. Not to diagnose them. But simply to wonder, *"What is life like for you?"*

Curiosity is what keeps us from jumping to conclusions or relying on assumptions. It invites us to set aside what we think we know and instead ask better questions. It's what turns *"Why are they acting like that?"* into *"What might be going on beneath the surface?"*

I use this a lot when people say something transphobic. Instead of shutting down or firing back, I try to ask myself: *Where is this coming from?*
If I can understand their point of view — even if it's uncomfortable — I might be able to gently turn it around. Sometimes that curiosity opens the door to a deeper conversation, one that wouldn't have happened otherwise.

In moments like those, you can't just bash against the wall. You'll only end up bruised. But curiosity gives you a way to move around the wall, or slowly take it down, brick by brick.

You can practice curiosity in everyday moments:

- When a coworker seems off or withdrawn — ask how they're doing, not just what's on their plate.

- When your partner is frustrated and you don't understand why — pause to ask, *"What's this feeling really about?"*

- When you encounter someone who believes something wildly different than you — resist the urge to debate and instead ask, *"How did you come to see things this way?"*

Curiosity doesn't demand answers. It simply makes space for people to be more than your assumptions about them.

Deep Listening

Once curiosity invites you in, the next step is listening — and not the kind we usually do.

Deep listening is the art of being fully present while someone else speaks.
Not listening to respond. Not waiting to jump in.
Just being there, open, focused, and patient.

We live in a world where we often listen just enough to reply or defend. But empathy asks for a different kind of attention — the kind where you aren't crafting your counterpoint in your head, but absorbing what's being shared.

That moment I mentioned earlier — when someone says something transphobic — that's where deep listening really comes into play. Curiosity helped me pause and ask why they might feel the way they do.

But it's listening that helps me actually hear what's underneath their words.

Sometimes it's fear. Sometimes it's misinformation. Sometimes it's just someone repeating what they've been taught, without ever knowing someone like me.

Deep listening for empathy isn't about winning the argument.
It's about being there. Being present. Hearing everything and taking it all in.
It's about allowing their perspective in — not to agree with it, but to try and understand it.

You can practice deep listening by:

- Putting your phone down and giving someone your full attention — even for just five minutes

- Not interrupting, even when you think you know what they're about to say

- Noticing tone, body language, or what's not being said, instead of just the words

This is especially powerful in moments of emotion — when someone is grieving, venting, or processing something difficult.
Often, what they need most is to be heard, not hurried.

Empathy begins with listening — not to fix or reply, but to understand.

Reflecting Without Judgment

The final — and often most difficult — part of empathy is sitting with someone's truth without rushing to judge, defend, correct, or compare it.

We all carry the urge to explain ourselves, to fix what feels broken, or to push back when something feels wrong. But empathy requires something gentler: the willingness to hold space for someone else's feelings, even when they clash with your own.

That same conversation I mentioned earlier — the one where someone said something transphobic — could have easily ended in a shutdown. Even after I got curious and listened deeply, there was still a moment when I had to choose:
Do I lash out?
Do I shut them down?
Do I get defensive?

Instead, I chose to reflect back what I was hearing. Not to excuse it, but to show them the impact of their words.

I said something like, *"When I hear that, it sounds like you're assuming that being trans is a phase, or that it's not real. That really stings, because my experience has been the opposite — it's been a long road to finally living as myself."*

I didn't attack them. I didn't try to shame them. I reflected what I heard and how it made me feel.

At first, they were confused. They hadn't even realized their words were hurtful.
But because I hadn't come at them with judgment, they were able to stay in the conversation instead of shutting down.

Reflecting without judgment doesn't mean staying silent or accepting harm. It means offering insight without the intent to punish.
It means staying grounded in connection, even when the moment is full of tension.

You can practice this by:

- Saying, *"I hear you saying* _____ *— can I share how that lands for me?"*

- Using "I" language to describe your feelings without assigning blame

- Taking a breath before responding, especially when your emotions flare up

Empathy is not silence.
It's presence.
It's the choice to stay in the room, even when it's uncomfortable — especially when it's uncomfortable — and respond with clarity, care, and courage.

Empathy doesn't grow from one big breakthrough.
It grows from small choices — moments of curiosity, quiet listening, and compassionate reflection — stacked together over time.

Empathy in Daily Life

Empathy doesn't require a grand gesture.
It shows up in the smallest, quietest ways.

It's in how you respond when someone's struggling — do you assume the worst, or wonder what's weighing them down?

It's in whether you pause before firing off a snarky reply.

It's in how you notice who's not being heard and make room for their voice.

But it's also in moments that don't always look like empathy.
It's the decision to stay calm when someone is short with you.
It's choosing to listen to a friend vent about something that doesn't affect you directly.
It's offering a moment of patience when a server gets your order wrong, or a coworker forgets a detail, or your child throws a tantrum at the worst possible time.

Empathy is what happens when you decide to make space for someone else's experience — even for a moment.

I remember being at my local Kroger and walking up to the checkout line just as a visibly shaken cashier was finishing a brutal interaction with a customer. The customer had let loose over coupons, out-of-stocks, and who knows what else — but none of it had anything to do with the cashier herself. She was just the person standing there when the storm hit.

I could have just smiled and moved on. But I'd worked in retail before — general merchandise, back when I was younger. So instead, I offered a little commiseration and let her talk it out. She needed to breathe. She needed to be reminded that not everyone was going to treat her like that.

I told her, *"I've been there too. People can be so much sometimes."*
And before I left, I said, *"I hope the rest of your day is worry-free."*

She softened. She exhaled. And maybe that one breath gave her a little more capacity for the next person.

Empathy lives in moments like that.

- When you check in on a friend who says "I'm fine," even though something in their voice tells you otherwise

- When you choose patience with a tired barista instead of frustration

- When you bite your tongue in an argument, not to let someone "win," but because you want to understand where the heat is coming from

- When you make room in a conversation for someone who keeps getting talked over

- When you hear someone say something that surprises or offends you — and you stay curious instead of defensive

These aren't heroic acts. But they matter.
Over time, these small choices shape your habits and how you show up for others.

Empathy becomes how you live, not just what you feel.

Your Story Makes You Human, Not Perfect

One of the biggest misconceptions about empathy is that it requires you to get everything right.

It doesn't.

You'll get it wrong sometimes.
You'll miss the point.
You'll say the wrong thing.

That's not failure. It's part of the process.

Empathy is not about perfection. It's about effort.
It's about choosing to learn, to apologize, to keep showing up after you stumble.

In my own life, I've seen how easy it is to get stuck worrying about whether you're saying the "right thing," especially when conversations feel charged or unfamiliar. But empathy isn't about perfect language. It's about being present, open, and willing to learn.

Your mistakes don't disqualify you from empathy.
They are the soil it grows in.

We don't build empathy by rehearsing scripts. We build it by practicing honesty, humility, and repair.
We build it by noticing when we've hurt someone — and choosing not to disappear in shame, but to step back in and say, *"I didn't mean to cause harm, but I see that I did. Thank you for telling me."*

Personally, I know I don't always get it right. I'm not only trans — I've also been diagnosed with ADHD. And like a lot of neurodivergent folks, I sometimes process the world by relating it to my own experience.
I compare stories as a way of connecting. I talk about myself to show I understand. But I've learned over time that what feels like empathy to me can sometimes land differently to others — like I'm centering myself or making the moment about me.

That's not my intent. But intention and impact aren't always the same.
So I've had to learn when to pause. When to let the silence hold.
When to remind myself: this is their moment, not mine.

And I'm still learning. Still catching myself. Still practicing.

The moments that have taught me the most weren't the ones where I said the perfect thing.
They were the ones where I didn't — but stayed anyway.

Where I paused and said, *"That came out wrong. Can I try again?"*

Or where I reached out after the fact and said, *"I've been thinking about what you said, and I want you to know I hear you now."*

Empathy is strengthened in the messy middle — when we fumble and reflect, when we let our discomfort lead us toward growth instead of retreat.

And just like no one expects a runner to be flawless the first time they hit the pavement, we can't expect ourselves to show up with fully-formed empathy every time we interact.
It builds with repetition, reflection, and repair.

So don't wait until you're perfect to practice empathy.
Start with who you are.
Start with the story you carry.
Start with your willingness to keep trying.

Because your story — honest, imperfect, and real — is what makes you human.
And it's your humanity that makes empathy possible.

Reflection

Before you move on, take a moment to reflect on and practice our skill:

- When was the last time someone truly listened to you? What made that moment feel safe or validating?

- Can you recall a recent time when you misunderstood someone? How might curiosity or listening have shifted that moment?

- Are there situations where you tend to react quickly or speak from your own story before holding space for others?

- What would it look like to practice empathy today — not perfectly, but intentionally?

Remember, empathy doesn't require a perfect script.
It starts with presence, awareness, and the courage to keep trying — even when it's messy.

The Power of Language

Language isn't just how we describe the world. It's how we shape it.

Language as a Reflection of Culture

Words aren't just neutral carriers of meaning. They come packed with assumptions, cultural context, and history. When we speak, we echo the past. The cultures we grew up in, the power structures we lived under, and the norms we never even thought to question are all embedded in our language. That isn't inherently bad, but it holds power.

Take words like *fireman, policeman,* or *chairman.* These terms assume men are the default. The structure itself reinforces an expectation. Even now, when many of us use "firefighter" or "chairperson," those older forms still linger. Language tells a story of who we've centered and who has been left out.

Sometimes, we try to rewrite that story.

Slurs are one of the most painful examples. I grew up in the '80s and '90s, and I heard plenty of them, especially from my uncles. The words they used weren't just insults. They were warnings. A reminder of what could happen if you stepped out of line.

Queer was around, but it wasn't the main one I heard. I don't think it carried the same sting where I lived, or maybe it had already started to shift. The ones that stuck with me were different. Harsher. Still echoing in locker rooms and internet comment sections today.

When I came into my identity, *queer* had already become more mainstream. It had been reclaimed by generations before me—activists, artists, and community builders who transformed it from an insult into something vibrant and inclusive.

By the time I stepped into it, *queer* felt like an open door. I didn't have to justify it. I could just walk through. It was flexible and familiar. It held space for the messiness and self-discovery that defined my experience.

In a way, I inherited that labor. Others took the heat so I could have the language. That's the gift of reclaimed terms. They don't erase the hard parts, but they make the next step a little easier for someone else.

Not every word has followed the same path. Some have fallen out of favor. The term *transexual* was once used with pride by many trans people. It shows up in older advocacy work, medical documents, and memoirs. At the time, it was the only word that captured what some people were going through.

Today, though, it often feels clinical or uncomfortable. Most of the trans community has moved away from it. Hearing it now can be jarring, even painful. The shift in how it's received creates tension, especially when revisiting older media that tried to make space using the best language it had at the time.

That's why something like *Rocky Horror* can be complicated. It was bold and transgressive, but the language it used now feels off. At the time, it helped crack open a door. Today, it makes some of us cringe. That tension between gratitude and discomfort is real.

Words evolve. They grow with us, and sometimes we outgrow them. That is what makes language powerful. It isn't fixed. It reflects where we've been, and it shapes where we're going. Every word we choose helps lay the foundation for what comes next.

Language as a Bridge (Not a Barrier)

Language can either open a door or shut it.

When someone uses the name you chose or gets your pronouns right without hesitation, it can feel like being handed a key to a space you weren't sure you belonged in. That kind of clarity and care says, "You're safe here. I see you."

When people get my pronouns right, it still catches my attention. Sometimes I expect *he/him* to slip out. After all, that was the default for so long. But then I hear *she/her* instead, and my brain lights up. It's a small thing, but it lands with weight.

And I wonder, are they being as intentional as I am when I talk to other transgender friends? Do they have to think about it? Or is it just natural now? Either way, it earns my respect. It makes me care about what they have to say.

The opposite is also true. When someone gets my pronouns wrong, especially in a way that feels careless, I find myself pulling back. I stop listening. I lose interest in their words. It's like the volume gets turned down.

I don't expect perfection. But I do expect effort. That effort builds trust. It tells me that I don't have to defend my identity in the space we share. You've already made room for it.

How something is said matters just as much as what is said. Tone and context shape meaning. The same phrase can sound warm and supportive, or it can sound dismissive and cold.

Compare, "They go by she now," said with curiosity and ease, to, "Whatever, I guess she wants to be called that now." The words are technically correct, but the tone shifts everything.

I grew up in a family that didn't often say what they meant out loud. Passive language and body language were the norm. What wasn't said often mattered more than what was. I learned to read the air and speak indirectly. I learned how to imply things, how to let silence carry meaning.

That's a skill I'm still trying to unlearn.

The hardest moments are when I'm upset—especially with my wife or my kids. I want them to just know. I want them to read my mood. That's when the old instinct kicks in. I hint. I sigh. I speak in a way that keeps my hands clean but leaves a mark.

I know it's not fair. But it's something I picked up early, and undoing that habit takes real work.

That's why I believe in being clear. Inclusive language isn't about finding the perfect words. It's about being intentional. It takes effort to say, "I'm feeling frustrated because I don't feel heard," instead of leaving someone to guess. It takes even more effort to say, "You matter, and I want you to feel that."

Don't expect people to read between the lines. Say what you mean. Be specific. Be kind.

That clarity builds trust. It tells people they don't have to constantly translate, accommodate, or wonder if they're wanted. It invites them in.

Harm in the Everyday

Language doesn't have to be cruel to be harmful.

Phrases like "you guys," "that's insane," or "are you even a real woman?" might seem small, but they stack up. They remind people that they don't quite fit the mold. Often, these are things people say without malice, but repetition wears down the edges of someone's identity.

Misgendering and deadnaming can be especially painful. Being called by a name you no longer use—or never chose—can shake your sense of self. It reminds you that who you are is either invisible or inconvenient to others.

Ableist language shows up everywhere, including in professional settings. We say things like "crazy deadline," "crippled system," or "blind review" without thinking. But these phrases reinforce the idea that disability is a flaw or an inconvenience, rather than a part of human diversity.

Even the systems we work in carry the weight of outdated thinking. Technical terms like *whitelist* and *blacklist*, or *master* and *slave*, still exist in parts of the tech world. These words weren't created to be cruel, but they reflect deeper structures of control, access, and hierarchy. Updating them isn't about erasing history. It's about making room for everyone to feel respected in their environment.

Idioms can be another hidden barrier. In multilingual teams or global workplaces, phrases like "hit the ground running," "bite the bullet," "kill two birds with one stone," or "drop the bomb" may feel natural to native English speakers, but they are often confusing or jarring to others. Many of these expressions have violent roots, pulled from war, hunting, or punishment. Their casual use reflects a cultural comfort with metaphorical violence that isn't universal.

Even among native speakers, idioms like "pull the trigger," "stab in the back," or "take a shot" can land differently depending on someone's personal experience. Trauma, neurodivergence, or cultural background can all shape how a phrase is heard. What's meant to be clever or punchy might come across as abrasive or unsettling.

Using idioms can also create an unintentional in-group dynamic where understanding them becomes a kind of social test. If you don't get the reference, you risk being seen as slow, unprofessional, or out of sync, even if you're fully capable. In that way, idioms don't just confuse. They exclude.

Saying what you mean provides clarity and removes the need for context. Idioms depend on shared understanding that many people may not have. Inclusive language favors connection, not cleverness.

People sometimes push back on these conversations, calling it "political correctness" or complaining about walking on eggshells. But inclusive language isn't about censorship. It's about connection.

Political correctness is often performative. Inclusive language is relational. It says, *I care enough to be clear. I care enough to include you in the conversation.*

When we make conscious choices about our words, we aren't just avoiding harm. We are creating spaces where people can belong.

When Words Feel Hard

It's okay to feel unsure. What matters is how you show up in that moment.

When someone shares something personal—like new pronouns, a name change, or an aspect of their identity you didn't expect—it's natural to feel caught off guard. You might be afraid of saying the wrong thing. You might not know what the "right" thing is. That's a very human response.

But silence can be more harmful than uncertainty. Avoidance communicates discomfort. And in that moment, the person sharing with you is already feeling vulnerable. They are giving you a piece of themselves and hoping you will handle it with care.

You don't need to know everything. You don't need to offer deep wisdom or profound support. Just acknowledge what's been shared. Be kind. Be curious, if invited. Be present.

Here are a few things that go a long way:

- "Thank you for telling me."

- "I appreciate you trusting me with that."

- "I'm glad you felt safe enough to share this."

- "I'll do my best. Let me know if I get something wrong."

- "Got it. Would you like me to correct others if I hear them slip up?"

If you mess up—and everyone does—correct yourself, give a quick apology, and move forward:

- "Sorry, she. Thanks for your patience."

- "I meant your new name. Thank you for correcting me."

What doesn't help is a long monologue about how bad you feel. When you say things like "I'm such a terrible ally," or "I always screw this up," it shifts the focus away from the person who needed support and onto your own discomfort.

This doesn't mean you can't feel awkward or upset with yourself. You can. But process that with someone else, later. In the moment, keep the spotlight on the person who trusted you with their truth.

If you are truly at a loss for words, even a simple "Thanks for letting me know. I might not get everything right, but I care about getting it right" can carry real weight.

And if you are not sure what to do next, it's okay to ask gently:

- "Is there anything you need from me right now?"

- "Would you like to share more, or would you rather just hang out?"

- "I'm here for you, whatever you need."

The point isn't to say something perfect. It's to say something human.

You don't have to be impressive. Just be present. That's what makes people feel safe. That's what creates connection.

That is the power of language. Used with care, it tells people they belong.

Reflection

The words we choose are more than just sound or text. They are signals. They tell the people around us whether we see them, whether we welcome them, whether we're safe.

And sometimes, they tell people the opposite, even when we don't mean them to.

I've had to unlearn a lot of the language I was raised with. Some of it was passive. Some of it was hurtful. Some of it was just confusing. But all of it shaped how I showed up in the world, and how the world responded to me.

Language is not fixed. It evolves. And so do we.

The beauty of inclusive language is that it doesn't require you to be perfect. It just asks you to be intentional. To be willing to grow. To notice how your words land and adjust when they don't serve the people around you.

Saying what you mean, clearly and kindly, isn't just good communication. It's an act of care. It tells someone, *you don't have to translate yourself to be here.*

That is how language becomes a bridge.

Let's reflect on what we've learned and ask ourselves a few questions:

- When was a time that someone's words made you feel truly seen or valued?

- Are there phrases or habits you picked up that you're working to unlearn?

- What kinds of language do you notice in your workplace or community that might exclude others unintentionally?

- How do you respond when you get something wrong? Do you center yourself or the person impacted?

- What's one small change you can make this week to be more intentional with your language?

Boundaries: Letting Go of the Why

A boundary asks us to trust, and allows someone to feel comfortable, safe, and seen, even when we don't fully understand.

How Boundaries Are Expressed

Boundaries come in many forms. Sometimes they're spoken. Sometimes they're shown through action, emotion, or energy. Learning to recognize each type helps us honor our own space—and the space of others.

Verbal Boundaries

A verbal boundary is usually spoken clearly and leaves little room for interpretation.

It might sound like:

- *"I need some time to myself."*

- *"I don't want to hug right now."*

- *"Please call me Jensen."*

- *"My pronouns are she/her."*

When someone shares a verbal boundary, they trust you enough to tell you directly what they need. Respecting a verbal boundary means hearing it and honoring it, without argument or pressure.

Physical Boundaries

A physical boundary is often shown through action rather than words. It's about creating personal space or protecting comfort.

It might look like:

- Stepping away from a conversation or crowded room

- Pulling back from a hug or choosing not to be touched

- Quietly leaving a loud gathering to find calm

- Moving a chair a little farther away in a crowded space

Christmas is a perfect example. The house is buzzing with noise, laughter, and kids running around.
You catch a glimpse of your cousin quietly slipping away through the din.
No big announcement. No apology. Just a small, quiet exit.

It can be tempting to call after them, *"Are you okay?"* or *"Can I help?"*
But sometimes, a silent exit is a boundary too—a way of saying *"I need space"* without words.

The most empathetic thing you can do is let them go. Trust them to take care of themselves, even if it leaves you with questions.

Emotional Boundaries

An emotional boundary protects someone's inner world—their feelings, memories, and sense of self.

It might look like:

- Changing the subject when a conversation gets too personal or painful

- Choosing not to share details about a private experience

- Saying, *"I'm not ready to talk about that yet."*

- Withdrawing or growing quiet when a topic becomes overwhelming

Emotional boundaries are about protecting what someone is ready—or not ready—to give. Honoring them means allowing people to hold their privacy without being pushed to share before they're prepared.

Energetic Boundaries

Energetic boundaries are the ones you feel more than you see.

They might show up as:

- A friend giving shorter answers when they need quiet time

- A coworker putting on headphones during a busy day

- A teenager withdrawing into silence during a noisy car ride

- A shift in body language, like crossed arms or less eye contact

These softer signals matter just as much as the spoken ones. Learning to notice them without demanding an explanation is an act of care.

Shaping Boundaries with Consent

At the heart of every boundary is consent. Consent is what makes a boundary real—not fear, pressure, or obligation.
It's worth repeating:

No means no.
A yes made in fear is not a yes at all.

Boundaries aren't just preferences. They are ways people protect their dignity, energy, and safety. When someone sets a boundary, they are trusting you to respect their space without bargaining, persuasion, or push-back.

Sometimes consent moments happen in small ways:

- A child gently pulling away from a hug, even when an elderly family member insists

- A family member tickling a kid who laughs, but then says, *"Stop"*

- A friend asking for quiet time during a lively conversation

- A coworker setting a limit like, *"I'm not available after 5 PM."*

- A teenager putting on headphones during a long drive to create a little bubble of their own

When we honor these everyday "no's," we practice something important. We learn to respect the person in front of us, without needing them to justify why they need space.
We teach ourselves that real consent is a living thing, happening every day, in every relationship.

The Challenge of Boundaries

Even when we know better, it can be hard not to take boundaries personally.

When someone pulls away, says no, or asks for space, it's easy to feel that pang of hurt.
Did I upset them? Are they mad at me? Did I do something wrong?

Sometimes the hurt runs even deeper.
We might feel like we aren't trusted by someone we care about, and that can be a painful thing to sit with.
It's hard when you believe you've earned someone's trust, and yet they still set limits you don't fully understand.

Not being fully invited into someone's private world can bring up sadness, frustration, even a sense of grief.
We want to believe that love, care, or loyalty should be enough to dissolve every boundary.
But real care also means allowing people to protect themselves when they need to, even if we don't get to know why.

Sometimes it plays out in small ways.
Maybe at Christmas, you noticed your cousin slipping out of the noisy room, and in that moment your instinct was to call after them, *"Are you okay?"* or *"Can I help?"*—instead of just letting them quietly exit.
Maybe they turned and said something like, *"I just need a little space right now."*

Even when someone sets a boundary with kindness, it can still leave a small, sharp ache inside—the quiet fear that you missed something important, or hurt them without realizing it.

It's a hard feeling to sit with, not because you did something wrong,

but because part of you wishes you could have made it easier for them.
And yet, that moment of discomfort doesn't mean you failed.
It simply means you care.

Caring doesn't require perfection.
It asks you to stay.
To trust their boundary even when your heart aches a little.
To let your feelings exist without making them the other person's burden to carry.

Your emotional reaction isn't wrong.
Feeling sadness, insecurity, or worry doesn't make you selfish.
It makes you human.

But your feelings are yours to hold.
They are not someone else's responsibility to fix.

Empathy means holding space for your own reactions without handing them to the other person to carry.
You can honor your feelings and honor their boundary at the same time.

Maturity in boundaries asks for courage on both sides.
The courage to set them, even when it's hard.
The compassion to respect them, even when they trigger something in us.

Empathy isn't about being perfect.
It's about standing in discomfort long enough to choose respect over reaction.

Sometimes the greatest act of love is letting someone have their space, even when a part of us aches to follow.

The Boundaries of Boundaries

There's an important truth about boundaries: real boundaries protect ourselves. They don't control others.

A real boundary sounds like:

- *"I need to step away if things get overwhelming."*

- *"I need time to process before I respond."*

It's a choice about what I will do to care for myself, not a demand about what someone else must do to ease my discomfort.

But sometimes, the word "boundary" gets stretched into something else.
It becomes a shield for control.
A way to manage others instead of managing ourselves.

It might sound like:

- *"If you really loved me, you'd stop talking to that person."*

- *"You have to call me by your old name or you're disrespecting me."*

- *"You aren't allowed to feel that way because it hurts me."*

These aren't boundaries. They're demands.
They are attempts to shape someone else's behavior to ease our own fear or pain.

Real boundaries start with ownership.
They say, *"Here is what I will do to protect myself,"* not, *"Here is what you must do to protect me."*

When you encounter someone trying to use a boundary to control you, you have the right to respond with clarity and kindness.

Nonviolent language and **I-statements** can help challenge control without causing more harm.

You might say:

- *"I respect your feelings, but I'm responsible for my own choices."*

- *"I hear that this is painful for you. I also need to honor my truth."*

- *"I'm willing to listen, but I cannot change who I am to make others comfortable."*

- *"I understand that this is hard, and I hope you can respect that I need to be true to myself too."*

- *"I care about you, but I can't sacrifice my identity to maintain this relationship."*

These aren't attacks.
They are invitations to stay in connection without losing yourself.
They are reminders that real empathy honors both people, not just one.

Real boundaries protect.
They don't possess.
And true empathy makes space for everyone to stand in their full humanity.

Trusting Without Knowing

Sometimes, respecting a boundary feels like standing in the dark.
You don't get the full explanation.

You might never know exactly why they needed space, and that's okay.

Empathy doesn't demand a full map before it trusts.
It simply says, *"I believe you."*
It trusts that someone knows their own limits better than we ever could.

When someone shares a boundary with us, the way we respond matters.

We can meet it with guilt or confusion, or we can meet it with care:

- *"Thank you for telling me what you need."*

- *"Take all the time you need. I'm here when you're ready."*

- *"I'm proud of you for taking care of yourself."*

- *"You don't have to explain. I support you."*

True empathy isn't always about sharing the same feelings.
Sometimes it's about standing beside someone, honoring what you can't fully see, and loving them enough to let them go when they need to.

Empathy is less about knowing and more about respecting.
It's about believing them, even when you don't have the full story.

In learning to honor the boundaries of others, we also come to understand the importance of honoring our own.

Reflection

- Think about a time when someone you cared about needed space. How did that moment feel?

- Were you able to trust their boundary without needing an explanation? What helped or made it harder?

- Have you ever mistaken someone's boundary for a personal rejection? What did you learn from that experience?

- How might you more gently recognize and respect emotional or energetic boundaries in daily life?"

- What language or self-reminders might help you respond more gracefully when boundaries are set?

Boundaries are not walls meant to keep us out.
They are doorways that say, *"If you want to walk with me, walk with care."*
When we honor those doorways without barging through, we build something deeper than closeness.
We build trust—the quiet knowing that even when space is needed, the bond remains.

Empathy begins in those moments.
Not in understanding everything, but in honoring everything anyway.

Allyship: Building Relationship Through Empathy

At the heart of every strong relationship is empathy.
Allyship is simply what happens when we let that empathy guide our choices, not just our feelings.

Allyship – Deepening Empathy with Relationship

Empathy doesn't stop once we understand someone's story. If anything, that's where it begins. We often talk about allyship like a status, something you become once you read enough, care enough, or attend the right workshops. But real allyship isn't a badge. It's a relationship. And like all meaningful relationships, it grows through listening, missteps, repair, and commitment.

Understanding is powerful. It opens the door. But allyship is what happens when we step through that door and choose to stay. It's what deepens when empathy is no longer just something we feel, but something we return to again and again through our choices.

Empathy Doesn't End with Understanding

After someone shares their truth, a common response is, "Thank you for telling me. I see you." That's a beautiful beginning, but what comes next? Allyship is the continuation of that empathy. It's saying, "I want to understand better," not just once, but as a practice. It means holding space for someone without demanding they relive their trauma for your education. It's recognizing that no matter how well you mean, it's not about you.

Empathy asks, "How does this feel for them?"
Allyship follows with, "How can I act in a way that honors what I've learned?"

It isn't about never making mistakes. It's about committing to relationship. A real ally isn't someone who always gets it right. They're someone who sticks around when they get it wrong.

From Witness to Companion

When someone lets you see their struggle, they are not asking for a performance. They are inviting you to walk with them. You don't need to lead the way. You don't need to narrate the experience. You just need to be there.

There's a quiet power in companionship. Allyship means recognizing when to speak and when to stand beside someone silently. Sometimes, just being present — without fixing, redirecting, or seeking credit — is the most empathetic thing you can do.

I remember a time a coworker noticed I had been misgendered during a meeting. Afterward, they didn't make a scene or pull me into an awkward apology. They simply followed up with the person who had made the mistake and offered a gentle correction. No drama. No spotlight. Just presence. That's allyship: choosing the relationship over the recognition.

Relationship-Centered Allyship

We often think of allyship as something public. But real allyship shows up in private, quiet, even unseen moments. It's not a performance of virtue. It's a relationship of trust.

This means allyship will look different in different contexts. Being an ally to a friend means something different than being an ally to a coworker or family member. But the through-line is consistency. It's not about grand gestures. It's about becoming someone who can be counted on.

As an introvert and often non-social person, I've always found that making and maintaining connections takes real effort. It's work. But the people who really know me — the ones who have built that relationship — understand that about me. Or I just say it out loud: "I kind of suck at this, but I care." That honesty, that transparency, can go a long way.

Understanding is a two-way street. In a relationship, you learn how someone shows up when they're being their true self — when they're not performing, just giving what they can. Sometimes support looks like showing up to an event. Sometimes it looks like a quiet check-in or a moment of kindness no one else sees.

Sincerity and transparency matter more than perfect wording or timing. Allyship that's rooted in empathy doesn't ask you to be polished. It asks you to be present. To show up as your raw self, even when it's awkward or imperfect, and say: "I'm here with you."

Allyship in relationship says:

- "I will try to understand you, even when it's hard."
- "I'll check in, not check out, when things get uncomfortable."
- "I care about who you are, not just what you represent."

This work is deeply personal. It's not always visible from the outside. But it matters.

You'll Get It Wrong — That's Part of the Relationship

If you stay in this work long enough, you will get it wrong. You'll use the wrong word. You'll misread someone's silence. You'll say something that lands in a way you didn't intend.

That doesn't make you a bad person. It makes you human.

What matters is how you respond. A strong ally doesn't rush to defend their intent. They lean into the relationship. They ask, "Did I hurt you?" or "Can I try again?" They resist the urge to make it about themselves. And they remember that repairing trust is more important than proving a point.

Empathy gives us the language to reflect.
Allyship gives us the humility to repair.

Repair Builds Trust

Mistakes are inevitable. Growth is not.

When we mess up — and we will — it's the way we respond that matters. Owning the harm, apologizing sincerely, and working to do better strengthens trust over time. It shows that the relationship matters more than pride or comfort.

But repair only builds trust if it's paired with learning. A pattern of repeated harm without change slowly erodes the foundation you're trying to build. If someone feels like they have to keep forgiving the same wound, it stops feeling like empathy and starts feeling like neglect.

Being human is okay. Being careless is not.

I think about a dear family member of mine who had a very hard time adjusting to my pronouns. It was even harder when I was using they/them. Some people really do have a tougher time — and early on, I had so much patience for that. But over time, the constant missteps, paired with excuses rather than simple corrections, started to hurt. It wasn't the mistakes themselves that made it harder to trust. It was the feeling that my identity had to wait for their comfort.

A simple correction, a little more awareness — that would have gone so far. Because repair isn't just about saying sorry. It's about choosing to honor someone's reality, even when it takes work.

And I'm grateful I stayed in that work with them. Through repetition, patience, and real effort on both sides, the missteps happen far less often now. And that family member has become one of my greatest allies — someone I am so proud to have walking beside me today.

Every apology isn't just a moment. It's a turning point. And when we choose to learn, we honor the relationship we're trying to protect.

Grow With, Not Over

There's a temptation to turn allyship into leadership — to speak for someone instead of with them. But empathy-centered allyship resists that urge. It lets people lead their own narratives. It doesn't take the mic. It holds space for the other person to speak.

You're not here to be the hero of someone else's story. You're here to walk beside them, learn from them, and grow with them.

The best allies don't need a script. They just need a willingness to keep learning, keep showing up, and keep the relationship at the center.

Because allyship isn't an identity.
It's a relationship.
And that relationship is built on empathy that never stops growing.

Reflection

Allyship is not a title you earn. It's a relationship you tend to. It's okay if it feels awkward or uncertain at first. The important part is that you stay in it. Keep showing up. Keep listening. Keep growing.

Here are a few questions to ask yourself as you continue deepening your empathy through allyship:

- **When someone opens up to me about their experience, do I listen to understand or to respond?**
  Am I giving them space, or filling it?

- **Do I wait for someone to ask for help, or do I offer quiet support before it's needed?**
  How do I balance showing up without overstepping?

- **When I get something wrong, how do I respond?**
  Do I center my discomfort, or do I focus on repair?

- **Am I willing to learn in private — not just perform support in public?**
  What would it look like to be a consistent ally, even when no one sees it?

- **How can I build trust through sincerity and transparency?**
  What would it mean to show up as my raw self — and let others do the same?

Allyship isn't about having all the answers. It's about being willing to ask the right questions, to grow in relationship, and to let empathy guide you — not just in moments of clarity, but in moments of confusion and challenge too.

You don't have to be perfect to be present.
You just have to care enough to keep showing up.

And over time, those small, imperfect acts of care can build something stronger than understanding. They can build trust.

Understanding and Repairing Microaggressions

Noticing the small harms is the first step toward healing them.

What Are Microaggressions?

There are things people say that never quite leave your body.

A sideways glance. A joke that leans just a little too close to the bone. A compliment that somehow sounds like an insult when you repeat it in your head hours later.

Most people don't mean harm. In fact, they usually insist they didn't.
"I didn't mean it like that."
"I was just joking."
"You know I support you."

But even when a blade is dull, it still cuts.

A microaggression is one of those cuts. Small, sometimes invisible, often unintentional, but still real. It's a comment or behavior that carries a deeper message, whether the speaker knows it or not: *You're different. You don't belong here. You're not quite right.*

I've heard them plainly:

- "You look really good—for a trans person."

- "You're so brave. I could never do that."

And I've heard them quietly, in the space between syllables. The way someone stumbles over pronouns. Or how they laugh a little too loudly at a joke about gender, waiting to see if I'll laugh too.

There was a time early in my transition—before the legal change, before the systems caught up with my name—when someone in a team meeting joked, "If I were going to be brave, I'd say a unicorn. Like Jensen. Magical and mythical."
Everyone laughed. I did too.

But I remember feeling the laugh catch in my throat.
What they thought was whimsical felt like a reminder that, to them, I was still somehow imaginary. A person who didn't quite exist in the same category as everyone else.

Sometimes, the hardest moments come from the mouths of children. They don't mean to be cruel—they're just piecing the world together out loud.
Still, when a kid looks at me and says,
"You have a boy's face," or *"How are you her mom if you sound like a boy?"*

These land. It's not malicious. It's not meant to hurt.
But it still does.

There's a different kind of ache that comes with those moments. Not because I blame the child—but because I see the world that taught them to question me in the first place.

Microaggressions aren't just about the words—they're about the way those words build walls around who we're allowed to be.

And the hardest part? Sometimes, you don't even realize you're bleeding until you're all out of bandages.

The Accumulation Effect

A single moment might not feel like much.

A joke. A question. A slip of the tongue.

But it builds.
It builds in the same way a pebble dropped into a backpack doesn't seem heavy until the pack is full of them. One stone is nothing. Ten are uncomfortable. A hundred will break your back.

That's what happens when you live with microaggressions.
They don't just sting in the moment—they linger. They return. They multiply. And after a while, the weight of them changes the way you walk through the world.

There was a week—not even a remarkable one—where I was misgendered three times. In Slack. In a hallway. In a meeting. All by different people. All well-meaning. All apologetic.

I told each of them, "It's okay." Because what else was I supposed to say?

But by the end of that week, I found myself avoiding eye contact. Wearing more neutral clothes. Speaking less. I didn't feel like Jensen— I felt like a flicker of myself, dimming.

I stood in front of the mirror one day and didn't recognize the version of me that looked back.
Not because I had changed.
But because I had started hiding again.

That's what the accumulation does.
It doesn't just wound—it erodes.

When You Mess Up: Repair Without Excuses

Here's the truth we all need to make peace with: you will mess up. I will too. We're human, and humans have messy wiring. Our mouths move faster than our awareness sometimes.

What matters isn't *if* we fail—it's *how* we show up afterward.

When our daughters were little, my wife and I taught them that a real apology includes two things:
"I'm sorry." And, "How can I help?"

It wasn't about forcing forgiveness or pretending nothing happened. It was about taking responsibility *and* offering care.

That's the same posture I hope for when someone says or does something harmful—even unintentionally.

You don't need a grand gesture. You don't need to overcorrect or turn it into a monologue about how hard it is to get everything right. You just need to mean it.

Once, during a project kickoff, a new colleague misgendered me during introductions. My heart sank, bracing for the usual clumsy recovery. But they just paused and said, "Sorry—*she*. Jensen, I messed that up. I'll make sure I get it right from now on."

Later that day, they messaged me privately:
"Thanks for your patience. I'm learning, but that's no excuse. Let me know if I ever say something off. I want to be better."

That was it. No defensiveness. No performative guilt. Just respect.

A good apology doesn't erase the harm. It meets it with enough humility to start healing.

When You Witness a Microaggression

There's another kind of moment that matters too, the one where *you're not the one harmed*, but you see it happen.

Those moments can feel like a test. Should you say something? Will it make things worse? Will it make people uncomfortable?

Maybe. But here's the thing: discomfort is not the enemy. Silence is.

That doesn't mean you need to swoop in and save the day.
It means you notice. You care. You choose to be someone who lessens the burden instead of watching someone carry it alone.

I remember a meeting where a colleague misgendered me. Twice. I was trying to decide whether to let it slide or speak up again when Lauren, my teammate at the time, gently said, "Jensen uses she/her pronouns."

That was it. Simple. Clear. No shame, no spotlight.

It gave the other person a chance to correct themselves without making it a big deal. But more importantly, it gave me a moment to breathe. To feel seen.

You don't have to be loud to be an ally. You just have to be present. To make space. To follow up. To let someone know, quietly or otherwise, *I noticed that too. You're not alone.*

Reflection

Microaggressions rarely show up as shouts.
They whisper. They echo. They linger.

They tell a story—not always the one we want to hear, but the one we carry.
And if you've been carrying a few of your own, I hope this chapter helped you feel seen.

We all want to belong. We all want to be understood. But sometimes, even the most well-intentioned words miss the mark—and what's left behind is the quiet hurt of being misunderstood, again.

Let's reflect on what we've learned and ask ourselves a few questions:

- Is there something someone once said to you—something small—that never quite left you? What made it stay?

- Have you ever said something you didn't realize was hurtful until later? What helped you see the impact?

- What happens in you when you witness someone being excluded, dismissed, or misunderstood? What keeps you silent? What might help you speak?

- When someone tells you you've caused harm, how do you tend to respond? What would it look like to stay open, rather than shut down?

- What habits—however small—could you practice to better support the people around you?

We won't always get it right. But we can always try again—with more intention, more awareness, and more compassion.

Maybe the real work isn't to be perfect.

Maybe it's just to stay open.

To keep showing up.

And when we fall short, to ask with our whole hearts:

"How can I help?"

Show Yourself Some Compassion

Self-compassion isn't just a nice idea. It's the ground we stand on when everything else feels shaky.

Remember Yourself

We learn so much about how to be kind to others. We give, and we give some more.
But sometimes, we need to give ourselves some of that same space, patience, and forgiveness.

Give yourself permission to be human — to rest, to set your own boundaries, to speak kindly to yourself, and to simply survive the hard days when that is all you can do.

Perfection Will Break You

Take a breath with me.

There's a voice in many of us that says, "If you can't do it perfectly, you're failing." It sneaks into advocacy work. It sneaks into healing. It sneaks into every part of being human.

Perfection is a lie. You don't have to get it right every time to be good. Mistakes are part of the path. Growth is messy. If you hold yourself to the standard of never making a mistake, you're setting a bar no human being can reach.

Real strength is being willing to learn out loud. It's choosing growth over guilt.

As an overachiever myself, I know how easy it is to put unbearable pressure on yourself to get things exactly right. Even when the people around you are supportive — even when they tell you it's alright — there can still be a voice inside that refuses to accept it.

Sometimes, when I find myself frustrated or snappy with someone, it's not really about them at all. It's about me. It's about the deep, aching feeling that I didn't succeed the way I wanted to. It's about the anger I turn inward when I feel like I fell short.

Those feelings are real. They deserve to be seen. But they don't have to be the end of the story.

Sometimes you have to set your ego aside and give yourself grace.
Believe the people who love you.
Believe your partner, your friend, your community when they say, *You are enough.*
Not because you earned it through perfection, but because you are human and you are loved.

Boundaries Are Not Walls

Breathe this in: You are allowed to protect your peace.

Setting boundaries is not about pushing people away. It's about creating space to show up more fully, more authentically, more sustainably.

Saying no is a kindness. It is an act of trust in yourself. It says, "I know what I need, and I respect myself enough to honor it."

Boundaries protect your energy. They protect your heart. And they teach the people around you that you are a person worthy of respect.

Communicating your needs is part of self-compassion.
It can feel vulnerable to say, "I need space," or "I need support," or even "I can't do this right now." But asking for what you need is not being rude. It is not a failure. It is a way of honoring your own humanity.

Everyone needs space sometimes. Space to breathe, to think, to come back to themselves. It is part of being human.

As a neurodivergent person, I sometimes need copious amounts of space. Certain noises, overwhelming environments, or unexpected disruptions can trigger a spiral of overstimulation. I've learned that when this happens — especially around crowded family gatherings like Christmas — the kindest thing I can do for myself and for others is to step away and work through it in my own time.

Being aware of your needs and communicating them clearly is not just helpful. It's essential.
A person who is practicing empathy with you will respect your request for space, even if they don't fully understand why you need it in that moment.
They don't have to feel it themselves to honor it.

Boundaries aren't selfish. They are the language of self-respect.

You Need Rest (No, Really)

Take another breath.

Rest is not something you earn by working yourself to the brink. It is not a reward for suffering. It is a basic human need.

You are allowed to rest simply because you are alive.

Rest can look like sleeping in. It can look like saying no to a commitment you don't have the capacity for. It can look like stepping away from the news cycle when the weight of the world feels unbearable.

But rest doesn't always mean sitting still.

For me, rest is sometimes riding my electric scooter.
The wind rushing through my hair reminds me of West Texas, where you either learned to love the wind or learned to fight it. I chose love.

There's something about the steady whoosh of the wind, the white noise it creates, that quiets everything else.
It gives me the space to let my thoughts spill out, to ride wherever my body wants to pilot me — balancing, breathing, moving forward without pressure.

Sometimes I ride past the neighborhood cats lounging in driveways.
Sometimes I dodge a few slow midday cars or catch the sun slipping down behind the rooftops.
It isn't about getting anywhere in particular. It's about creating space inside myself.

Rest can be stillness.
Rest can also be movement that feels free, that brings you back to yourself.

Taking care of yourself is not selfish. It's essential.

Talk to Yourself Like Someone You Love

Let's go even deeper now.

Pay attention to the voice in your head. Notice how you speak to yourself when you struggle, when you fall short, when you're simply having a hard day.

Would you speak that way to someone you love?

If the answer is no, it's time to rewrite the script. Gentleness is not weakness. Compassion builds strength. Treat yourself the way you would treat a beloved friend, because you are just as deserving.

My transition taught me a lot about this.

Before I came out, I was so used to speaking harshly to myself that I hardly noticed it anymore. I would mess up a small thing — drop my keys, forget something — and mutter, "Damn you" under my breath. I thought it was normal. I thought it was harmless.

When I changed my name, I started noticing something strange.
When I was kind to myself, I called myself by my new name — Jensen. But when I messed up or felt frustrated, my old name would slip out. It was like all my self-deprecation was still tied to the person I had been trying so hard to survive as.

It showed me something I hadn't realized before:
I wasn't just changing my name.
I was changing the way I treated myself.

My "rebirth" — my becoming — gave me a second chance to speak to myself with kindness. It wasn't instant. It wasn't perfect. But slowly, I began to replace the old habits of self-criticism with new habits of compassion.
I began to forgive myself for being human, instead of punishing myself for it.

One of the most powerful tools I found was practicing self-affirmations — even when they felt awkward.

It might sound hokey. I get it.
But if you have lived a life filled with self-deprecation, there is a lot to unpack.
You won't believe the good things about yourself if you never hear them — not even from yourself.

Get a deck of affirmation cards. Print out little sayings you love and tape them next to your mirror. Write a kind note to yourself in a notepad every morning. It doesn't have to be fancy. It just has to be honest.

Another thing I did for myself — and it changed my life — was take selfies every day for over a year.

I wanted that self-confidence.
I wanted to like me for who I am.
Not just in my mind, but in what I *saw*.

Taking selfies wasn't about vanity. It was about learning to look at myself without tearing myself apart.
It gave me permission to say, *"I look great today."*
And when it didn't feel quite right, it also gave me room to say, *"What if I tried something different next time?"* — without anger, without shame.

It was about *seeing myself* through a lens of love and curiosity, not judgment.

Self-affirmations, selfies, mirror notes — they are not about pretending you have it all figured out.
They are about reminding yourself every single day:
I am worthy of love.
I am proud of how far I've come.
I am still becoming, and that is beautiful.

Because the truth is, rebuilding your relationship with yourself changes everything.

If you don't like yourself, it becomes very hard to truly like others.
The lens you see the world through gets clouded with cynicism and bitterness.
You stop seeing goodness — in yourself, and in the people around you.

Loving yourself isn't selfish. It's how you keep your heart open.
It's how you make room for hope, for joy, and for empathy — not just for yourself, but for everyone you meet.

When It Feels Like Too Much

There will be days when getting out of bed feels like an accomplishment.
There will be days when brushing your teeth, answering a message, or making yourself a meal will feel like moving mountains.

That doesn't make you weak. It makes you human.

We live in a world that measures worth by productivity, by how much you can achieve in a day, how much you can push through.
But the truth is, your worth was never meant to be measured in checklists or milestones.

Some days, the bravest thing you can do is simply exist.
Breathe.
Feed yourself.
Rest.

Some days, you won't be the person who tackles everything. You'll be the person who quietly tends to the tiny flame inside you — the one that refuses to go out even when the wind howls.

Those days matter too.

You are not a failure because you need to move slower.
You are not a burden because you need time.
You are not broken because you cannot meet the impossible expectations you once set for yourself.

On the days when it feels like too much, give yourself the grace you would give a dear friend.
Speak to yourself softly.
Allow yourself the space to simply be.

Survival is not just existing.
Survival is an act of courage.
It is a quiet, stubborn kind of hope that says, *I am still here.*

And maybe, yes — it reads a little like a cat poster.
But maybe that's the point.

Maybe you need to hear it the way the world whispers to you through a silly little poster:
"Hang in there."
Because if you can just make it through today, tomorrow is a world of possibilities waiting for you.

You are enough.
You were always enough.

Reflection

Take a moment to breathe and reflect.

- What is one small way I can be kinder to myself today?
- Where in my life am I expecting perfection instead of growth?
- What boundary could I set to better protect my energy?
- How can I communicate one need clearly and kindly this week?
- How can I give myself permission to rest, without guilt?
- What would I say to a friend who was feeling how I feel right now?
- How can I remind myself that surviving is a form of strength, too?

Remember:

Some days we survive, and that's enough.

A LETTER TO YOU

If you've made it here, I want you to know something simple:

I'm proud of you.

You stayed with me through these pages, through the stories, the hard moments, and the quiet ones. You opened your heart to experiences that might not match your own. That takes a kind of bravery we don't always talk about, but it matters.

When I first started writing this book, it was because people kept asking me the same questions.
How should I act around someone who's transgender?
What should I say?
How do I avoid messing it up?

And every time, my answer was simple:
Give a little space.
Bring a little empathy.
Come with good faith, and I can meet you there. I can be an open book if you come with kindness.

That's really what this book is — a way to help you listen a little differently.
To help you see people as people, even when their story looks different from your own.

Yes, my journey as a transgender woman is woven into these chapters.

But this was never just about being transgender.
It was about being human.

It was about learning how to show up for people even when you don't
have all the answers.
It was about giving grace, making mistakes, trying again.
It was about practicing empathy like a muscle — something you build,
one choice at a time.

I hope you think about the moments we walked through together.
The kid trying on hope in the mirror.
The mother explaining two moms at a kindergarten table.
The worker carving out space for kindness in a world that moves too
fast.

And I hope you remember — your moments matter too.
Your story matters.

Maybe someday you'll tell it.
Maybe someday you'll be the reason someone else feels seen when they
needed it most.

If you ever come back and reread these pages, I hope you'll see them
in a new light.
I hope you'll notice not just my story, but the heartbeat underneath
it — the reminder that behind every face is a life, a journey, a whole
world you might not see at first glance.

If you carry anything with you from this book, let it be this:

- You don't have to fully understand someone to treat them with kindness.

- You don't have to agree with every part of someone's path to honor their dignity.

- You don't have to be perfect to make a real difference.

You just have to be willing.
Willing to listen, willing to try, willing to make space for the stories you haven't lived yet.

Thank you for walking this road with me.
Thank you for believing that a softer, braver world is possible — and that it starts with us.

You don't have to do it all at once.
You just have to start.

One story at a time.
One choice at a time.
One act of empathy at a time.

I'll be out there too, trying right alongside you.

With all my heart,
Jensen

Reader Resources

Whether you're here to deepen your understanding, support someone you love, or grow into a more empathetic version of yourself, these resources can help. Some are practical, some are emotional—but all of them are about connection, reflection, and learning with care.

Books

- *Advice From Your Trans Aunty* by Erica Vogel — A gentle, honest collection of advice and affirmations from a trans woman to anyone navigating identity, belonging, or the complexities of being human.

- *How to They/Them* by Stuart Getty — A friendly, funny guide to pronouns and gender-neutral language.

- *This Book Is Gay* by Juno Dawson — A candid and inclusive guide that breaks down identity, attraction, coming out, and queer life with humor and honesty.

- *Gender Queer* by Maia Kobabe — A graphic memoir exploring gender identity and self-discovery, told through powerful visuals and heartfelt storytelling.

- *Sorted* by Jackson Bird — A warm, witty memoir that highlights the author's trans experience and journey toward self-acceptance.

- *Love That Story* by Jonathan Van Ness — Essays that blend humor, vulnerability, and insight, offering a window into life beyond the binary and the power of radical self-love.

- *Pageboy* by Elliot Page — A deeply personal memoir chronicling the author's experience coming out, transitioning, and reclaiming his voice.

- *Nonviolent Communication* by Marshall B. Rosenberg — A transformative guide to speaking and listening from the heart, offering tools for empathy, understanding, and deeper connection.

Children's Books on Identity and Affirmation

- *Red: A Crayon's Story* by Michael Hall — A blue crayon mistakenly labeled as red discovers the importance of being true to yourself.

- *Julian Is a Mermaid* by Jessica Love — A joyful, beautifully illustrated story about identity and unconditional love.

- *I Am Jazz* by Jessica Herthel and Jazz Jennings — Based on the real-life experience of Jazz Jennings, this book introduces what it means to be transgender in a gentle, affirming way.

- *When Aidan Became a Brother* by Kyle Lukoff — A warm story about a young trans boy preparing to become a big brother.

- *They She He Me: Free to Be!* by Maya & Matthew Smith-Gonzalez — A celebration of pronouns and self-expression for all identities.

- *It Feels Good to Be Yourself* by Theresa Thorn — A clear, accessible explanation of gender for young readers and their grownups.

- *My Shadow Is Pink* by Scott Stuart — Explores gender expression and the strength to be yourself.

- *My Shadow Is Purple* by Scott Stuart — Embraces non-binary identity and celebrates living in-between or beyond categories.

- *Neither* by Airlie Anderson — A whimsical story about not fitting into binaries—and finding a place where everyone belongs.

- *Not Quite Narwhal* by Jessie Sima — A gentle metaphor for discovering that you're different—and exactly where you belong.

- *I Like Myself!* by Karen Beaumont — A vibrant, joyful affirmation of self-worth. Love who you are, just as you are.

Documentaries & Films

- *Will & Harper* (2024) — A road trip documentary about friendship and transition, featuring Will Ferrell and Harper Steele. Honest, funny, and deeply moving.

- *Disclosure* (Netflix) — A powerful look at the history of trans representation in media, told by trans creatives.

- *The Death and Life of Marsha P. Johnson* (Netflix) — A tribute to one of the most influential Black trans activists, and an investigation into her legacy.

- *Paris Is Burning* — A landmark documentary about ballroom culture, queer joy, and chosen family.

- *Becoming More Visible* — Follows four trans young adults navigating identity, visibility, and resilience.

- *The Danish Girl* (2015) — A dramatized story of Lili Elbe. While not without critique, this film meant a lot to me—especially in how it portrays love and authenticity in partnership.

- *Bill Nye Saves the World – Season 1, Episode 9: "The Sexual Spectrum"* (Netflix) — A science-based look at gender and sex as spectrums. (Fair warning: there's a mid-episode musical number that's... skippable. But Nye's closing remarks are absolutely worth it.)

Podcasts

I'm not an avid podcast listener, but these come highly recommended and align closely with the themes of empathy, identity, and listening with care.

- *Gender Reveal* — Weekly interviews with trans and nonbinary guests, plus thoughtful commentary on language, policy, and community.

- *We Can Do Hard Things* — Hosted by Glennon Doyle. Not trans-specific, but often dives into identity, parenting, and authenticity.

- *TransLash Podcast* — Hosted by Imara Jones, centering trans voices, culture, and social justice.

Websites, Articles & Interactive Tools

- Erica in the Morning
  https://www.ericainthemorning.com — Honest, educational reflections on trans life and current issues—from someone living it, not just reporting on it.

- Genderbread Person
  https://www.genderbread.org/ — A visual framework for understanding gender identity, expression, sex, and attraction as distinct (but connected!) axes.

- Practice With Pronouns
  https://www.practicewithpronouns.com/ — Helps you practice gender-neutral pronouns in realistic examples.

- Pronouns.org
  https://www.pronouns.org/ — A guide to understanding and using pronouns respectfully.

- Them
  https://www.them.us/ — A digital publication with news, stories, and essays by and for LGBTQ+ people.

Support & Advocacy Organizations

If you or someone you love is looking for community, support, or a way to get involved, these organizations are a good place to start—especially if you're in Texas like me.

First and Foremost: A Texas Treasure

- TENT (Transgender Education Network of Texas)
  https://transtexas.org — A trans-led, grassroots organization doing powerful work in education, advocacy, and community building. If you only visit one link today, let it be this one.

National Organizations

- Trans Lifeline
  https://translifeline.org — A peer-led hotline offering emotional and financial support to trans people.

- The Trevor Project
  https://www.thetrevorproject.org — 24/7 crisis support and mental health resources for LGBTQ+ youth.

- PFLAG

https://pflag.org — Support and education for families, allies, and LGBTQ+ people.

- GLAAD
  https://www.glaad.org — Amplifying LGBTQ+ voices and promoting fair representation in media.

- Human Rights Campaign (HRC)
  https://www.hrc.org — Advocacy, education, and legal protections for LGBTQ+ individuals.

- Transgender Law Center
  https://transgenderlawcenter.org — A trans-led legal advocacy organization fighting for justice and equality.

Additional Texas-Based Resources

- Equality Texas
  https://www.equalitytexas.org — Legislative and community advocacy for LGBTQ+ Texans.

- Out Youth (Austin)
  https://www.outyouth.org — Safe spaces and support services for LGBTQ+ youth and families.

- The Mahogany Project (Houston)
  https://www.mahoganyproject.org — A Black queer and trans-led organization offering care, connection, and resources.

- Transgender Wellness Center of Houston
  https://www.montrosecenter.org — Mental health and wellness services for trans folks, hosted by The Montrose Center.

- Resource Center (Dallas)
  https://www.myresourcecenter.org — A North Texas hub

for LGBTQ+ support, legal resources, and gender-affirming services.

A Note About External Resources

All links in this section belong to their respective creators, authors, or organizations. I have included them because I believe they offer valuable insights or tools, but I did not seek permission or affiliation to feature them here. The views expressed on these websites may not always align with my own, and the content may change over time. URLs were accurate at the time of publication, but if any are no longer active, you can find the most up-to-date list at https://findingjensen.com/resources.

Acknowledgments

Writing *Finding Jensen* has been one of the most personal, vulnerable, and rewarding experiences of my life. It would not have been possible without the love, support, and encouragement of many remarkable people.

To my wife, Amanda — my partner in every sense — thank you for your fierce love, steady support, and belief in me when I needed it most. And to my kids, who have been my biggest, loudest, and most joyful advocates — your pride in me has carried me farther than you know. You remind me daily what it means to live authentically and unapologetically.

To my therapist — thank you for suggesting journaling as a tool for reflection. I know this book wasn't exactly what you meant, but that encouragement helped me find my voice in a whole new way. Honestly, everyone should have a therapist. A good one helps you grow, advocates for your well-being, and helps you reflect — sometimes in unexpected and life-changing ways.

To the coworkers and friends who said, "You should publish this" — thank you for planting the seed. Your encouragement helped turn a private story into something I could share out loud.

To Kelly and Wendy — thank you for helping me take care of and keep track of our communal cat. Seriously, the best cat moms!

To the trans and queer community — this book is for us. Your visibility, courage, and everyday existence make space for stories like mine to be told. I'm proud to walk alongside you.

And to every reader who picks up this book with an open heart —
thank you. My hope is that it helps you grow in empathy, connection, and compassion, and that you leave these pages with a deeper
understanding of others — and of yourself.

About the Author

Jensen Chappell (she/her) is a transgender writer, software engineer, and DEI leader based in Texas. With a career rooted in technology and a passion for building inclusive culture, Jensen brings both heart and insight to her work—whether she's leading engineering initiatives or advocating for belonging in the workplace.

Her debut book, Finding Jensen: A Path to Empathy Through Understanding, weaves personal narrative with practical reflections on identity, language, and connection. Drawing from her lived experience as a trans woman, a parent, and a culture-shaper in tech, Jensen invites readers to understand the power of empathy—not just as a concept, but as a skill that changes lives.

When she's not writing or coding, she's probably following her cat Ume on her next adventure around the neighborhood, cheering on her family at taekwondo, or watching a intriguing series on TV while having coffee with her wife, Amanda. She believes every story told with honesty is a step toward making the world a little kinder.

Learn more or get in touch at https://jensenchappell.com.